THE

HARPER
ESTABLISHMENT;
OR,
HOW THE STORY BOOKS ARE MADE.

NEW YORK:
HARPER & BROTHERS, PUBLISHERS.

PREFACE.

THIS series of Story Books, though they are intended to be written in a simple and lucid style, so as to bring them within the comprehension of all, are by no means designed exclusively for children. The subjects of many of them will be such that they can only be appreciated by minds that have attained to some degree of maturity, and are accustomed to habits of careful and patient thought.

The subject of the present number, the great Printing Establishment of the Harpers in New York, is one of this class; and though I have endeavored to make my description sufficiently full in its character, and simple in its details, to be intelligible to every class of readers, I have made no attempt to bring it down to the capacity of children. The older and the more thoughtful of the sons and daughters of a family may derive great instruction from the perusal of it, especially if they are assisted by the explanations of the father and mother as they read, but the younger ones must expect to find it above their reach. They had their turn in the Story of Timboo and Fanny.

I have taken great pains to make all the statements contained in the work in respect to all the structures, machines, and processes described strictly exact, so that gentlemen in the interior of the country, who take a practical interest in subjects connected with mechanical science, may rely on the correctness and accuracy of the information which this account furnishes. In these efforts I have been greatly assisted by the various gentlemen who have had the charge of the several portions of the work of constructing the edifice, as well as those who are now employed as overseers in the different processes of manufacture. 1 have been especially indebted to the following named persons not only for information obtained from them, in the first instance, in respect to the various branches to which their responsibility extends, but also for their assistance in the careful revision of my descriptions and statements after they were written :

JAMES BOGARDUS, Engineer, constructor of the iron front of the building.

JOHN B. CORLIES, Architect and Builder.

JAMES L. JACKSON, designer and manufacturer of the iron columns and girders.

ABRAM S. HEWITT, of the firm of Cooper & Hewitt, manufacturers of the iron beams.

CONTENTS.

ENGRAVINGS.

ENGRAVINGS.

HARPER ESTABLISHMENT.

CHAPTER I.

GENERAL STRUCTURE OF THE EDIFICE.

THE buildings of the Harper Establishment are situated in New York, on Cliff Street and Franklin Square. The establishment covers about half an acre of ground, and consists chiefly of two blocks of buildings, one fronting on Cliff Street, and the other fronting on Franklin Square, with a court between. The two blocks of buildings are united, and made, as it were, one, by a series of iron bridges connecting the various stories of the two blocks with each other and with a large circular tower in the court, which contains the common stairway for the whole establishment. The edifice is constructed almost exclusively of stone, brick, and iron, and is as perfectly fire-proof as the present state of architectural science and art can make it.

The frontispiece represents that portion of the building which fronts on Franklin Square. It is five stories in height, with a cellar and sub-cellar below, making seven floors in all. The front is built wholly of iron. It consists in each story of twenty-one Corinthian columns, with lofty windows filling the intercolumniations. Each range of columns supports the bases of the range above, and thus they rise, tier above tier, to the topmost story.

Over the entrance-door is a full length statue of Benjamin Franklin in iron. Between the windows of the fifth story, too, is a row of smaller statues of Washington, Franklin, and Jefferson. Above them is the cornice of the roof, supported by massive trusses. There is no entrance in the front of the building for the receipt and delivery of goods. The place for this business is in the court-yard between the two buildings, which is entered by a passage-way from Cliff Street. Thus the front of the building is never encumbered with carts or drays coming to or leaving the establishment, nor are the sidewalks obstructed with bundles of paper or boxes of books.

There are two cellars under this block, one of which is, however, entirely out of ground on the back side, where it fronts the court-yard. The depth of the foundation of the edifice may be inferred from the fact that the floor of the lowermost cellar is twenty-two feet below the sidewalk. A large portion of the space in these cellars is used for the storage of paper. This paper is taken across, as fast as it is wanted, into the lower stories of the building on Cliff Street by a subterranean railway under the court. This will be more particularly explained by-and-by, when we come to the engraving of the court-yard.

There are no staircases leading from one story to another in either of the buildings within the walls, but there is one common staircase for the whole establishment in the round tower already mentioned, which has been built for the purpose in the court-yard.

Thus the several floors of the buildings are continuous and entire throughout. This construction is adopted as a safeguard against fire; for, as there are no openings through the floors, and as the floors themselves are built of brick and iron, and are thus completely fire-proof, no fire can be communicated through them in any way. The staircase in the tower is connected with each story of both buildings by iron bridges, and is found to be amply sufficient for all purposes. This, also, will be particularly explained when we come to the history of the court-yard.

Thus, with the exception of the great staircase ascending from the entrance-door in front to the counting-room, which will presently be described, all the floors are continuous throughout—of solid brick and iron—and thus the spread of fire among the contents of the buildings from floor to floor is rendered impossible. There is, indeed, nothing but the contents of the buildings that can burn, for the edifices themselves are constructed, almost without exception, of materials entirely incombustible.

The height of the stories, and the general magnitude of the scale on which the whole building is constructed, may be appreciated by comparing the edifice with the ordinary four and five story buildings on each side of it in the engraving. The general counting-room is in the centre of the building on this front, in the first story above the principal basement. The access to it is by a very broad staircase—twelve feet wide—ascending from the centre door. You will see the top of this staircase, and the interior of the great counting-room into which it opens, in the engraving on the next page. Besides the counting-room, this building contains the *stock* and

View of the interior of the counting-room.

THE COUNTING-ROOM.

stores of the establishment, consisting of vast quantities of paper and other materials in the cellars and on the lower floors, and books by hundreds of thousands in the various stages of manufacturing stock in the stories above. The extent and the arrangement of these vast magazines will be hereafter described.

The engraving on the opposite page represents the counting-room. The view is taken from the back side of the room, looking forward. The staircase is seen in the centre, coming up from the great door on the Franklin Square front, as seen in the frontispiece. We see a person just ascending the stairs, near the top. The three other sides of the opening through which the stairs come up are inclosed by a strong and ornamental balustrade.

In the background of the picture, which represents, of course, the front side of the room, there is a rectangular space, about forty feet by fifteen, inclosed by a railing, which may be considered the counting-room proper. Here are the desks and seats of the proprietors of the establishment, with sofas and chairs along the sides of the inclosure for visitors, or persons having business with the proprietors personally. This area is the constant resort of booksellers, authors, artists, travelers, and persons of distinction from every part of the United States, and, indeed, from all quarters of the world. The four brothers Harper, the original founders and present proprietors of the establishment, are almost always to be seen here, engaged in their various duties, such as receiving reports and listening to inquiries from the various mechanical departments, issuing orders, answering questions, holding consultations, considering new projects, waiting upon authors who come to offer manuscripts, and artists who bring in drawings or engravings, and in other like occupations. It is an animated and busy scene, though the arrangements are so complete and convenient, and the space so ample, that there is no bustle or confusion. A vast deal of very important business is transacted here, and often by men of high distinction both in the literary and business world; but it is transacted with few words, and in a very prompt and decisive, though very quiet manner.

Without the railing, on each side of the staircase, are several desks. Four of these are seen in the engraving. They are placed so as to face toward the centre of the room. They are occupied for the various departments connected with the book-keeping and accounts, and for business connected with the city trade. Beyond these, and still nearer to the foreground, are other appointments and fixtures. On the right are cases for exhibiting samples of books. There are two of these cases in different positions. One stands with its front toward us, showing us the books which it contains. The other has its back toward us. We see a lady and two gentlemen standing by it, examining the books. A clerk stands near one of the gentlemen, and seems to be conversing with him. On the left we see a large iron safe.

The cases above referred to are only intended for the purpose of showing specimens of the books which the house publish, as a guide to booksellers and others in making up their orders; for very little retail business is done at this establishment—none, in fact, except as a matter of convenience and courtesy to individual purchasers. The business of the house is almost exclusively the publishing of books to be sold in quantities to booksellers. The general stock, therefore, does not consist of individual copies of books arranged on shelves as in a library, as is usual in ordinary book-stores, but of *quantities* packed in bins, with specimens only in the show-cases below. We see a portion of these bins on what seems to be the side of the room on the right. It is not really the side of the room, however, which appears in the engraving, but only a double block or tier of bins built up from the floor to the ceiling, to furnish receptacles for the books. This block of bins is two stories high, as seen in the engraving. Access to the upper story is obtained by means of a gallery, which extends along the whole length of the block. We see men upon this gallery bringing books down to be packed and sent away. There are two openings like wide doorways through this construction to another part of the room, which is surrounded on all sides by bins. On the left-hand side of the room the arrangement is the same, though it is not shown in the engraving. Indeed, only about three quarters of the length of the apartment itself is shown, there being the same space between the range of columns on the left and the range of bins forming the partition, that there is on the right, though this space in the engraving is cut off on the left side. This space is twenty feet, and the whole length of the part of this floor of the building which is inclosed between the two ranges of bins is eighty feet. The depth of the apartment from front to back is seventy-five feet. Beyond, on both sides, are wings, which are entered through the openings in the ranges of bins above described, and which extend, including the depth of the bins, about twenty-five feet farther, making the whole front one hundred and thirty feet. There are four openings leading to these wings, two on each side. The number of bins on both sides of this great hall, including those within the two inner compartments, is about one thousand, and each one is of sufficient capacity to hold nearly one thousand ordinary duodecimo volumes.

The back part of the room, a small portion of which only is seen in the foreground of the engraving, is occupied for the purpose of filling orders for books, packing the books in boxes and bundles, mailing the subscribers' copies of the Magazine and Story Books, keeping sundry accounts, and other similar purposes. It is from this place that the vast issues from the establishment are daily made. The boxes and bundles are wheeled, when made up, out through a door in the rear of this part of the room, which conducts across the court by an iron bridge to the hoist-way, where the steam-engine takes them, and lets them gently down to the cart or wagon waiting in the court below. We shall see the arrangement of this mechanism more particularly when we come to the court. But the relative position of the packing-rooms, the bridge, and the hoisting, will be seen on the plan on the adjoining page.

The plan represents the first or principal floor of each building, namely, the publishing and counting-rooms of the Franklin Square building, and the great press-room in the Cliff Street building. The former is on the right, as seen in the engraving; the other on the left.

At the extreme right of the Franklin Square room is seen the counting-room, between the head of the staircase and the front of

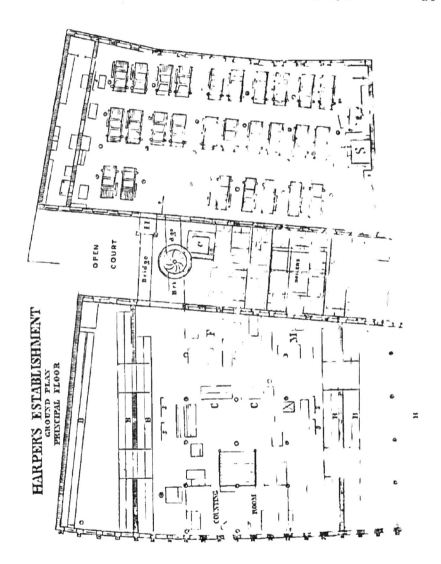

HARPER'S ESTABLISHMENT
GROUND PLAN
PRINCIPAL FLOOR

the building.   The desks and other furniture are represented on the plan.   There are two entrances to the inclosure, one on each side of the great staircase, and the space itself is only separated from the rest of the apartment by a railing, as shown in the perspective view on a previous page.

On the other side of the staircase, toward the centre of the apartment, is the area marked C, which is appropriated to the city trade.   It is very convenient for this purpose, being easily accessible from the entrance to the building.   The area is partially inclosed by desks, safes, counters or cases for the exhibition of samples of books, and other similar furniture.   These objects are represented in the plan, but they can be seen still more distinctly in the perspective view.

At the back side of the room, near the centre, is the area marked F, devoted to the business of receiving and answering foreign orders.   Here are large tables for assembling and packing books, and desks for keeping the accounts, and trucks for drawing away the boxes and packages, when they are made up, to the door leading to the hoist-way, which is close at hand.   There are two doors, indeed, leading to the court, near this part of the building.   One opens upon the bridge that conducts to the hoist-way, the other to the one that leads to the staircase in the round tower, and thus to all parts of the Cliff Street building.   These two bridges are seen in the plan.

To the right of the space devoted to the foreign trade, looking toward the back side of the room, is another inclosure, marked M on the plan, which is appropriated to the work of mailing periodicals. The great business at this place is, of course, the mailing of the subscribers' copies of the Magazine.

On the north and south sides of the apartment may be seen the ranges of bins, marked B, B, B on the plan, surrounding two inclosures of the form of wings. These bins consist of ranges of very strong shelving, about five feet deep, separated by a solid brick wall, which forms the back of the rows of bins. The partitions extend from the floor to the ceiling. The upper tiers are reached by galleries, as seen in the perspective view. The open court, marked in the plan, is accessible by carts through an arched passage-way in Cliff Street. This passage-way is not shown on this plan, being on the story below the one here represented. The two walls inclosing it are, however, seen at the end of the Cliff Street building. The position of two of the bridges, the hoist-way, H, the circular tower, the great square chimney, c, as well as of the glass roof that covers the boiler-room, are shown in the plan. A perspective view of this court-yard, with a more full account of the various objects which it contains, will be given in a subsequent chapter.

The plan shows the arrangement of the presses in the great press-room of the Cliff Street building. This room is on the principal story, that is, the first above the basement. The other floors of this building are all appropriated to the various mechanical operations connected with the printing and binding of books. They will be described hereafter. In the mean time, a view of the front of this portion of the edifice is given on the next page. The opening where we see the cart going in is the entrance to the court.

View of the front on Cliff Street.

VIEW OF THE CLIFF STREET FRONT.

CHAPTER II.

THE FIRE-PROOF FLOORS.

THE great difficulty in the construction of fire-proof buildings is the work of making the floors. Walls may easily be built of brick or stone, but wood alone has been considered hitherto, until within comparatively a short time, almost essential for floors; since for floors, which must necessarily, to so great an extent, sustain themselves, with as little support as possible from below, there is required a degree of strength and lightness combined which has hitherto been found to exist in no other material.

It is true that architects have long been accustomed to build floors of brick or stone by supporting them on arches, which rest on columns or walls in the room below; but these arches, on any mode of construction heretofore adopted—at least until within a few years—have required columns or walls to support them so massive and solid, that the room below was necessarily encumbered with obstructions, and made, indeed, almost useless, in order to furnish support for the floors of the rooms above. We see this construction in the basement stories of the old and central portions of the Capitol at Washington, the New York Exchange, and in such buildings as the Pantheon in Paris. In all these and similar buildings, the basement story is rendered dark, and gloomy, and dungeon-like by the immense number and massive forms of the walls, piers, columns, and groined and vaulted arches, necessary to support the floor of the principal story above. Then, again, above this principal story, in such buildings, there could be usually nothing; for the rooms in it, if large, as in most cases they must necessarily be, could only be kept free from obstructions similar to those below by some vast roof or dome for a covering, constructed at great expense, and rising necessarily so high as to preclude the possibility of having any useful apartments above it.

All this, however, was of no very serious consequence in the case of churches, and other similar structures, where the dungeon-like basement might be used as a *crypt* for tombs and other such purposes, and where, also, the very nature of the edifice required that all the space above the principal floor should be occupied as one story. It was very different, however, with such buildings as are required for the practical purposes of modern mechanical arts. In these cases, what is necessary is to divide the whole height of the building—fifty or eighty feet, perhaps—into many distinct stories by floors made as thin as possible, so as to economize space, and each self-sustaining, so as not to encumber the story below it with supports. To do this with wood has been easy. But wood is highly combustible. How to do it with any incombustible material has long been a great desideratum. The object was at length finally accomplished, and the first successful construction by the new method, as at length perfected, is the edifice we are describing. Indeed, it was in the construction of this edifice that the method was perfected.

If the reader will turn back to the engraving of the counting-room in page 16, and look up to the ceiling, he will readily under-

General arrangement of the columns and girders

stand the mechanism of these floors, for the whole structure is there almost entirely exposed to view. You observe three rows of columns extending through the room from front to back. These columns support a range of ornamental girders, the mechanism of which will be hereafter explained. Each one is essentially a cast iron arch, the lower ends of which are connected by a rod of wrought iron. The form of it may be likened to a *bow* of cast iron, with a wrought iron *string*. Upon the girders, and extending from one row of pillars to the other, there rest the ends of a range of *wrought* iron beams. The double lines seen in the engraving in the ceiling, running from left to right, from one range of columns to another, represent the lower edges of these beams. The beams themselves, by means of broad flanges wrought on the lower side of them, support a series of flat brick arches, which extend from one to another of them, and thus furnish a continued bearing for the flooring above. The upper surface of the arches, when the masonry was completed, was leveled by filling up the spandrels with grouting, strips for nailing the floor-boards to having been previously laid for the purpose, and then the whole was covered with a wooden floor.

Thus the whole structure consists simply of a series of long, narrow, flat brick arches, supported by wrought iron beams, the ends of the beams being supported in their turn by girders of wrought and cast iron, and these by a range of cast iron columns, supported by a similar range in the story below.

The whole system is accurately represented in the following drawing.

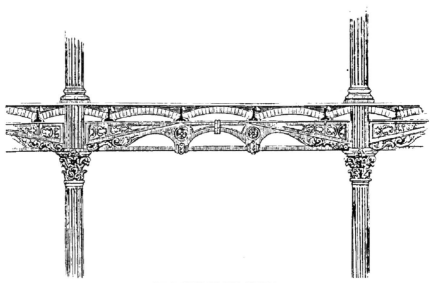

MECHANISM OF THE FLOORS.

The round rod connecting the ends of the girders is the tension-rod. It is of wrought iron. It acts as a tie-beam to prevent the two ends of the girder from spreading by the pressure of the weight on the arches above. These rods are two and a half inches in diameter. The whole mass of iron lying between the tension-rod and the range of arches above forms the body of the girder, and is cast in two parts, one for each side, the line of division being at the centre. These parts correspond in their function to the rafters of a roof, while the tension-rod answers to the tie-beam. The tendency of the weight resting on the floors above is to crowd the centre ends together, and to force the lower ends of the girder apart, thus bringing a heavy lateral strain upon the tension-rod. Indeed, it is on the power of the tension-rod to resist this strain that the whole security of the structure depends.

Were it not for the action of these tension-rods, the lateral thrust, as it is termed, of the girders—that is, the tendency to spread at the base, in consequence of the pressure of the weight above, would come upon the heads of the columns, and thence would be communicated from girder to girder to the sides or ends of the building, being increased in its passage by the lateral thrust of all the girders in the line. This would produce a pressure against the walls of the building which it would require an enormous thickness of the walls to resist. As it is, each tension-rod counteracts the lateral thrust of its own girder, and thus every thing is independent and self-sustaining.

The cast iron part of the girder appears somewhat complicated in its form, but it is very simple in its functions, which is, in fact, precisely that of a pair of rafters in a common roof. As to its form, any intelligent mechanic whose attention may be attracted to this drawing will observe that the leading outlines of the form are. determined by the necessity of increasing the strength and thickness of the iron in those parts of the girder where the great strains would come. The pattern is ornamented, too, with great judgment and taste. These ornaments are, on the whole, not expensive, since, as the girders are cast, and a great number are thus formed from one pattern, the expense of carving the pattern is widely distributed.

The girders are of different sizes in different parts of the buildings, on account of the different distances of the ranges of columns that support them. They vary from five hundred and forty pounds to eight hundred and sixty each for the cast iron part. The tension-rods weigh about two hundred and forty pounds each.

But let us now return to the drawing. Above the girders, and resting upon the iron beams, the ends of which are seen represented black in the drawing, are the brick arches. These arches are about four feet span, that being the distance of the beams from each other, and are four inches thick. They extend, of course, in length, from one range of columns to another, usually from eighteen to twenty feet. The form of the beams is seen in the section shown in the engraving. The ends rest in chairs, which are cast upon the upper side of the girder. The form and position of these chairs, and the manner in which the ends of the beams rest in them, is also shown in the engraving.

In building the arches, the bricks were not laid in mortar, but were placed in their positions dry, and then grouted with hydraulic cement.* For this purpose, water-tight centres were made to support the bricks below while the arch was in process of building, and then the grouting was poured between the bricks. When the arches were completed, the spandrels were filled up with concrete to the level of the crown of the arch, and then a floor of narrow yellow-pine plank, one inch and a quarter thick, was laid over the whole. The planks of the floor are tongued and grooved together,

* Grouting is the process of pouring liquid mortar into a mass of masonry previously laid dry, so as to fill the interstices, and to cement the whole into one solid mass

and blind-nailed, in the best manner, to strips of wood laid previously in the concrete. The ends of these strips are seen in the drawing, by the side of the ends of the iron beams. They are dovetailed into the concrete, to prevent the possibility of their rising.

The floors are thus lined with wood, with a view to the health and comfort of the persons employed in the establishment. A wooden surface is found to be much more convenient and agreeable to the tread than any that can be formed of masonry or metal. A surface of brick or stone, too, by keeping the feet cold, exerts an injurious influence on the health, and makes the persons who use it, especially if they sit much at their work, always uncomfortable. These plank floors may, indeed, be considered as a wooden carpet laid over the brick floors.

It was necessary that the floors for an edifice destined to such purposes as this should possess great strength. In one room, for example, the floor is loaded with a weight of *one hundred and fifty tons of presses.* In the paper-room the weight is still greater, there being sometimes nearly twenty tons of paper on a space ten feet square. Paper, when lying in compact masses, is exceedingly heavy. It weighs about thirty-five pounds to the cubic foot. The floors, however, are calculated to bear a burden of from three hundred to five hundred pounds to the *square* foot ; that is, they would be probably safe for five hundred, but are absolutely certain for three hundred. This would allow of covering the floor all over with stacks of paper ten feet high, or to fill the room full of men as close as they could stand, *in three or four tiers, one over the other.* Indeed, some engineers have considered that the construction has been made unnecessarily strong.

I was somewhat surprised, on making a calculation with the architect, at the statistics of this fire-proof flooring. The number of cast iron columns and girders—similar to those shown in the drawing of the counting-room—in both parts of the edifice, is over two hundred and fifty. This, too, does not include the eighty exterior columns in the front of the building on Franklin Square. The number of brick arches, averaging about four feet span, and fifteen feet in length from girder to girder, with wrought iron beams to support them, is about two thousand, and the whole area of floors thus supported in the different stories is between two and three acres. Let a farmer in the country select from among his fields a two and a half acre lot, and imagine the whole surface of it floored over, at a height of twelve feet above the ground, with a series of brick arches, supported by two hundred and fifty cast iron columns below, and covered above with a very close and compact yellow-pine floor, and he will have some idea of the magnitude of the scale on which this vast structure is planned.

CHAPTER III.

MANUFACTURE OF THE IRON BEAMS.

THE construction of the floors described in the preceding chapter, by means of wrought iron beams, and by light segmental arches thrown from beam to beam, is a very important feature in the construction of these edifices. It is novel also, these edifices being the first in which the principle has been thoroughly tested. The nature and character of these beams, therefore, and the mode by which they are manufactured, deserves especial notice, particularly on account of the economy which they are the means of introducing in the structure of fire-proof buildings, both in respect to the cost, and to the space which the floors occupy.

It is no new thing to build a fire-proof structure, but it is a new thing to build one at a cost which places this desirable result within the means of all who build in large cities. It is estimated that the loss by conflagrations in the United States amounted to twenty-five millions of dollars during the year 1854. This sum would easily pay the interest on the extra cost of making fire-proof all the structures in the country in the manner here described. Besides, the mere loss in dollars does not cover the disastrous consequences of this vast destruction of property. The domestic misery and moral degradation which inevitably result from such sudden and overwhelming calamities are beyond pecuniary estimate.

Iron was early proposed as a substitute for the arches or masonry originally employed, because it could be placed horizontally, like wooden beams, and would cost less than the stone-work. In a beam, however, the essential requisite is that it shall be *stiff* enough to sustain the load. To secure this quality, the beams must be of a depth proportioned to the width of the space they are to cover. For all ordinary purposes, this requisite involves great weight of iron in each beam. It is well known that many tons of cast iron can be melted and formed into a single piece:

10   C

but cast iron is comparatively too weak to resist a transverse strain, which is the peculiar strain produced on a beam by a loaded floor. To be perfectly secure, then, with cast iron, it was necessary to use a much larger quantity of material than would be required of wrought iron. The cost was thus increased to such an extent as to confine the use of such beams to a really limited sphere. Besides, cast iron is liable to flaws, a single one of which might endanger the safety of an entire building. It also has another peculiarity, namely, that by being repeatedly loaded and released from its load, some internal change is produced in the texture of the iron, which weakens it, so that it has less power each time to resist the strain than before; and hence, in floors subjected to great intermitting strains, the ultimate failure of the cast iron beams is certain, if the loads approach nearly to the measure of the strength of the material. The total destruction of some large buildings and bridges in England led to the investigation of the cause, and to the establishment of the facts above stated.

Attention was next turned to wrought iron. Wrought iron has all the properties necessary for a beam in far greater perfection than cast iron. It does not break suddenly, but, when *overstrained*, gives notice of the approaching failure by slowly bending. It is much stronger than any other material to resist a transverse strain, and therefore may be made proportionately light, thus saving weight in the walls and foundations of the building, and head-room in the respective stories. Patient experiments were made to determine the best form in which to distribute the material. The highest mathematical knowledge and skill were required to determ-

Flanged beams of wrought iron proved to be the best

ine the laws which governed the strains upon wrought iron, and it is one of the proudest triumphs of modern science that a few short months only were required to determine finally and forever, on scientific principles, the laws of construction for cast and wrought iron, which the blind experiments of centuries before had failed to discover.

For building purposes, it was finally settled that flanged* beams of wrought iron are most desirable when the requisites of strength, lightness, and convenience of application are considered. This point being determined, it was necessary to devise the best mode of producing beams in this material. Two modes of working wrought iron are known, one by hammering it, the other by *rolling* it into the required shape. Hammering is an expensive operation, and is found to make the beams too costly for use. Flanged beams of the requisite weight had never been rolled. In fact, the whole process of rolling iron is comparatively new. It was invented by Cort in the last century, who, by his invention of the puddling process as well, did more than any other man, except Watt, for modern industry, and was rewarded with poverty in his lifetime, and is now almost forgotten in the grave. To him is due the manufacture of iron at a cost which enables it to be used with such profusion in the mechanic arts, thus greatly cheapening all the artificial necessaries of civilized life.

The difficulty of heating and handling heavy masses of iron,

* A flange upon a beam is a flat projection extending from end to end of it. A good example of a flange is seen in the projecting rim of a rail-road wheel, which serves to keep the wheel from running off the track.

though a very serious one at first, was nevertheless overcome long before any practicable process could be devised for making bars deep enough, with flanges broad enough, to answer for spanning any considerable distance between walls. Hence, to use wrought iron at all, it became necessary to rivet separate pieces together into the shape of a flanged bar. But, as separate pieces are never as strong as a single piece, and as the rivet-holes necessarily diminish the strength of the material, it becomes necessary to use more iron, besides expending great labor in fastening the pieces together. This made the beams expensive, and, although fireproofing now became practicable, and free from most of the objections which could be urged against the other modes, it was still too costly for ordinary purposes, owing to the complex character of the beams.

The desideratum was therefore to make a solid rolled flanged beam of the right shape and proportions, and of the weight required for the spans ordinarily adopted in the buildings of large cities. The method of rolling such flanged beams was finally brought into successful operation at the iron-works of the Trenton Iron Company, situated in Trenton, N. J. The difficulties to be overcome in contriving and constructing the necessary machinery were very great. The mass of iron required for each beam, and which has, of course, to be pressed through the rollers at almost a white heat, is enormously heavy. Then the difficulty of constructing the rollers so that the iron, in passing through between them, shall have formed upon it flanges so wide as are necessary for beams, was very serious. We can not here describe the means by which at length the end was attained.* The arrangement was invented by a young Englishman named William Borrow. He was a relative of the author of Lavengro and of the Bible in Spain. Mr. Peter Cooper, under whose general charge the operation was conducted, was specially interested in the work, from the desire to employ such beams for the purpose of making fire-proof the large edifice which he was then erecting in New York for the Scientific Institution. He calculated that he should be able to put up the machinery in four months, and at an expense of about thirty thousand dollars.

The difficulties were, however, found to be far greater than had been foreseen. Instead of four months, it was two years before the machinery was brought into successful operation, and the cost of it, instead of thirty, was a hundred and fifty thousand dollars. And when at length the machinery was made to work successfully, the designer, Mr. Borrow, suddenly became ill, and died within a week, from the prostration of all his energies, mental and physical—a martyr to the difficulties which beset the practical workers of the world, whose story is seldom told, and who die without odes or funeral orations to celebrate their triumph or to honor their memory. And yet it is very likely to prove in the end that William Borrow has been one of the benefactors of his race. His invention will probably save millions of property from destruction—will ward off sorrow and calamity from innumerable hearths and

* The process of rolling out these immense bars of glowing iron forms a very magnificent spectacle. It can be witnessed at any time by visiting the works at Trenton, which are always readily shown to strangers.

homes; and, by the preserving of capital from destruction, give vigor to great industrial enterprises in many future years.

It was just about the time that the machinery for rolling these beams was brought to perfection that the Messrs. Harper were making arrangements for the erection of the new buildings for their establishment, and, after giving the subject a careful consideration, they determined to adopt them.   The result has been triumphantly successful, and this mode of building is now likely to be extensively adopted.   After a full and careful examination of the subject by the government, it has been decided to adopt the plan in all the custom-houses and other public edifices in the United States.

A wrought iron beam of this principle seems a very simple thing, both in its structure and in its functions, and yet it is surprising what a vast combination of means and instrumentalities is necessary, and on what a prodigious scale the work must be performed, in order to produce such beams with sufficient economy to make the invention of practical value to society.   It has already been stated that a solid wrought iron beam might be made by hammering, but that its cost, if thus manufactured, would be too great to allow of its use.   The expense would, however, in this case, be incurred in the *process of manufacturing* rather than in the *original outlay* for machinery.   An outlay of twenty-five thousand or thirty thousand dollars would enable solid hammered beams to be made, but then the expense of the process of manufacturing would bring the cost to ten or twelve cents per pound.   Rolled beams are made at five or six cents per pound, or about one half

Great investment of capital required in the manufacture

the above rate. But then the expenditure of capital required in the first instance, in order to effect this reduction, is enormous. In the first place, in order to make iron cheaply, the works must be on a large scale. This precludes the use of charcoal as a fuel, because it can not be got in quantities sufficiently large for great works without soon driving the woodchopper to a distance from the works so great as to destroy the value of the coal by the expense of hauling it. Mineral coal must therefore be used, and some site of manufacture must be selected to which both ore and coal can be conveniently brought in large quantities. Then extensive blast furnaces must be erected for the conversion of the ore into pig metal, and a forge built for turning the pig metal into wrought iron by the processes of puddling* and rolling.

The works of the Trenton Iron Company are upon the smallest scale which will combine all these processes in an economical manner, and yet the total expenditure for mines, furnaces, mills, water and steam power, in establishing them, is about one million of dollars. The number of hands employed directly are about two thousand, and the labor of all these is essential to make a single beam at six cents per pound. Besides this, the coal-mines must be opened and operated on an extensive scale, in order to produce coal cheaply. At least a million more is essential for this purpose; for, although the iron-works do not take all the coal, yet, if the mines were not operated extensively, the coal would not be cheap enough to enable the manufacturer to make beams cheaply.

* Puddling is a peculiar process by which cast iron is converted into wrought iron by means of passing it between rollers at a great heat

Then the coal and ore must be got to the works. This is accomplished by the Lehigh Canal and the Morris Canal, which have cost some twelve or fifteen millions of dollars, and are maintained by a large annual expenditure. Then the pig iron must be transported to the mill over works that have cost two millions of dollars more; and, finally, the beams must be brought to New York either by the Delaware and Raritan Canal, or by the Camden and Amboy Rail-road—works which have cost some ten millions of dollars more, thus making essential for the production of a single rolled beam at six cents per pound, instead of a hammered one at ten cents per pound, an investment of from twenty-six to thirty millions of dollars, which, though of use for countless other purposes, is still essential for this purpose; for if a single link in the chain were wanting, the extra cost would more than cover all the difference between the hammering and the rolling of iron.

This simple statement will serve to explain why the comforts and luxuries of life are made accessible to all ranks by modern industry, while only two hundred or three hundred years ago they were confined to a very small portion of the community. Whenever any article can be made on a scale sufficiently large to take advantage of the best method, it can be cheaply made; when but little is required, the cost must be great. Hence, in the progress of society, manufactured articles will be brought within the means of all when all require them.

CHAPTER IV.

INTERIOR OF THE CLIFF STREET BUILDING.

THE edifice on Franklin Square is mainly devoted, as has already been explained, to the purpose of storing paper and books, and the various other supplies of stock and materials used in the establishment, while the processes of manufacture are carried on altogether in the Cliff Street building. In order to give the reader a distinct idea of the arrangement of this building, and of the manner in which the different floors are appropriated to their several uses, the artist has drawn a sectional view of the edifice, representing at one view the whole interior of it. By turning over the leaf this engraving will be seen. It represents the seven floors of the building, with the operations which are performed in each. I propose, in this chapter, to take, with the reader, a cursory survey of the whole, with a view of afterward considering the several operations by themselves, one by one, and describing them in full detail.

The lowermost story seen in the section is the basement. At the extremity of it, on the left, we see parts of the engine and machinery which supply moving power for all the operations of the establishment. This power is conveyed to the different floors by a system of axles, pulleys, and bands, extending from story to story. The main work which this engine has to perform is the driving of the presses on the floor above.

Sectional view of the Cliff Street building.

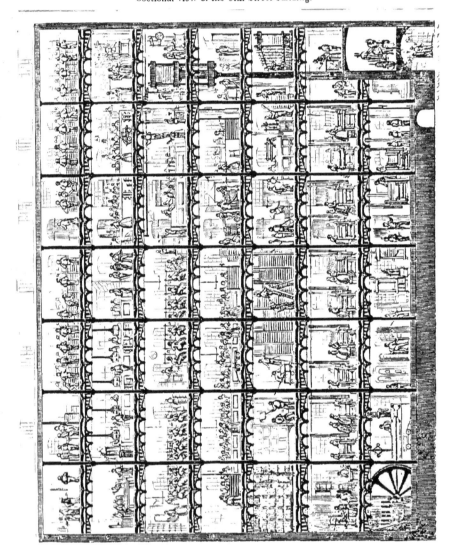

Farther toward the right, in the basement story, we see a door which leads to the boiler-room in the court-yard. Farther still, near the centre of the room, several hydraulic standing-presses are seen, and also, still farther to the right, some printing-presses. The principal use of this lower room is to receive the paper from the store-room in the Franklin Square building, and prepare it to be put upon the printing-presses in the room above. It requires to be pressed in the standing-presses in order to make it smooth, and to be damped that it may take the ink properly from the impression. Of course, only a very small portion of the operations performed in this room can be shown in a section like this. The room is, in fact, more than sixty feet wide from front to back, while the section shows only a single line of operations from left to right through the centre of it. At the very extremity of the room on the right, we see a door which leads to the subterranean vaults, where the electrotype and stereotype plates are stored. Still farther to the right, beyond the partition wall at the end of the room, we see a horse and cart coming from the court through the arched passage-way, and directly beneath is a section of one of the vaults, with two men going into it by the light of a lantern.

The first story above the basement, which is the principal or first story of the building, is the great press-room. This is the room which is represented in the ground plan on page 21. There we saw the position of the presses on the floor: here, on the other hand, we have a front elevation of one tier of them. There are three tiers, ten in each tier, except two spaces opposite the doors, making twenty-eight in all. The weight of these presses is about five tons each, making ten tons for the two which stand between each two of the columns. The distribution of these columns, and the arrangement of the girders and arches on each of the floors, is very distinctly seen in this sectional drawing.

We observe that each of the presses is attended by a girl, who stands upon a raised platform by the side of it. Her duty is to *feed* the press with paper, placing one sheet at a time. The sheet is thrown over when it is printed by what is called the fly, which is a light wooden frame, like a hand with a multitude of straight slender fingers, which lifts the sheet when it has received the impression, and throws it over upon the pile formed by those which had been printed before. At the right-hand end of the room this fly may be seen very distinctly in the act of going back after another sheet of paper, and on the other presses along the line we see it in various positions, bringing the printed sheet over.

At the extreme end of the press-room, toward the right, we see two men standing at a table. They are preparing a form for the press. This is a very important operation, and will be, hereafter, more fully described. Near them is a flight of steps leading up to an elevated compartment directly over the passage into the court-yard, where we see the horse and cart coming out. This is the office of the foreman of the press-room. Over his desk is a large opening, through which he can survey his whole dominion, and observe the action of all the presses and machinery. The men who are employed in preparing the forms for the press are directly beneath this window.

At the other end of the press-room, namely, at the extreme left, is a hand-press, used for working off hand-bills, circulars, and for other small operations.

We now pass to the next story above, which is called the dry-ing and pressing-room. The printed sheets, as fast as they are taken from the presses below, are brought to this room through the hoistway in the court-yard. The entrance to this hoistway is seen opposite the third press in the press-room, counting from the right toward the left. It is a wide opening closed by double doors, and directly above it, in each story, is a similar opening lead-ing to the hoistway. In one of the stories the doors are open.

The range of doors leading to the staircase in the tower is a little to the left of the openings leading to the hoistway. The doors leading to the staircase are narrower, it will be seen, than those of the hoistway. All the other openings in all the stories are windows.

But let us return to the drying and pressing-room. At the ex-treme right, over the office of the foreman of the press-room, is a range of hydraulic presses, where the sheets are pressed after being printed. They are, however, dried before they are pressed. This drying operation is performed at the other extremity of the room, namely, on the left. There is a compartment inclosed here which is kept constantly heated by steam-pipes, with a system of large frames, like horses for drying clothes, which can be drawn in and out. We see the compartment in the engraving in the first divi-sion of this room on the left, that is, in the part between the wall and the first tier of pillars. Between the first and second tier of pillars we see two of the frames out. One of them is already filled with sheets of paper, and the workman is in the act of pushing it in to the heated compartment, in order that the sheets may be dried there. The other frame is not yet ready to go in; a workman is employed in putting sheets upon it by means of a pole with a cross-bar at the top, as seen in the engraving.

When the sheets are dry, they are taken on trucks—one of which is seen standing near—to the other extremity of the room, to be pressed in the hydraulic presses. An enlarged view and a more full description, both of the drying apparatus and of the hydraulic presses, will be given in a subsequent chapter.

The hydraulic *engine*, by which the pressure is applied to the sheets and the presses, is represented in the engraving, though I am not certain that the reader will be able to find it. It stands in the division of the room which comes between the first and second columns, reckoning from the right. It stands near a window, a little to the left of where two men are at work piling up a stack of paper to go into one of the hydraulic presses. To the left of the hydraulic engine is a range of tables—only one of which, however, is seen in the engraving—where the sheets are prepared to go into the presses, and arranged when they come out. The operation, which is quite a curious one, will be more fully described hereafter.

In the centre of the room are to be seen, stacked up in large racks, a number of great piles of sheets of paper that have been pressed and dried, and are now ready to be folded for the binder. These stacks are some of them so high that, in order to put on the uppermost sheets, the men are obliged to mount upon ladders, as seen in the engraving, and the weight is very great which comes upon the girders and beams of the floor below.

The next story above, namely, the third above the basement, is called the folding-room. The principal operation performed in it is that of folding the sheets of paper after they are pressed, and preparing them to be stitched or sewed. The work of folding is performed by girls, who sit at long tables arranged in the room for this purpose. One range of these tables, with the girls at their work, is seen represented in the engraving, occupying the left half of the apartment. Gas fixtures, at proper distances, are suspended over the table for evening work in winter. Similar burners are to be seen in various other parts of the building.

Near each end of this table is to be seen an apparatus presenting the appearance of a frame of parallel bars, rising to a height of two or three feet above the floor. These are sets of steam-pipes, by which the apartment is warmed. Similar sets of pipes are seen in various other places on the different floors.

At the time of folding the sheets, it is necessary to insert, in their proper places, between the leaves, all such engravings as have been printed separately from the body of the work. The case of shelves seen at the end of the apartment, on the left, near the end of the table, is used to contain supplies of these engravings, arranged for use.

The doors leading to the hoistway are represented open on this story, and some men are in the act of drawing in a load of printed sheets from the platform. A part of the machinery of the elevator is seen through the opening.

To the right of the hoistway door, in the fourth story, near the right-hand end of the apartment, is seen a massive structure, forming a base for the support of heavy presses in the room above. These are hydraulic presses of great weight, and a special support was accordingly provided for them, consisting of extra columns in the second and third stories, resting on a very thick wall coming up from the stories below. These presses are used for pressing the folded sheets, so as to bring them together into a compact form, ready for sawing the backs and binding them. There are two of these presses in fact, though only one of them is shown in the section. The hydraulic pump by which the pressure is applied is seen to the right of the press, near the end of the room. A little to the left of the press is a small machine called a sawing machine, which will hereafter be more fully explained. The man on the ladder, to the left of the sawing machine, is engaged in making some adjustment of the machinery that runs along from end to end of the room, under the ceiling, to supply motive power to the various engines in the apartment. The remainder of this apartment is occupied by girls seated at long tables, and employed in the work of sewing or stitching the sheets. A clock is seen hanging upon the wall, opposite the centre of the tables. A little to the left of the clock is the desk of the man who superintends these operations.

The next story, that is, the fifth above the basement, is called the FINISHING-ROOM. The various operations performed in this room will be described in detail hereafter. The foreman is seen sitting at a desk, on an elevated platform, in the last division but one toward the right. We see the clock on the wall behind him. Before him are a large number of men engaged in what is called *forwarding* the books—that is, preparing and fitting the covers, pasting down the fly-leaves, trimming the edges, and performing other such processes preparatory to the stamping and gilding. On the extreme right is a row of standing-presses, used for pressing the books after they are sewed and put together, this making the fourth time in which the books, or the materials of which they are composed, have been subjected to pressure in the different stages of the manufacture. The number of presses required for all these varied operations is not less than twenty-five. Of printing-presses—all massive machines of great power, and driven by steam—there are thirty-three in the principal press-room and in the story below.

In the back corner of this apartment, toward the right, is an inclosure for the process of marbling. Other portions of the room, toward the left, are also inclosed for different processes of finishing work. In the first division on the left, we see the men engaged in sprinkling the backs of the books for the purpose of producing the mottled appearance often seen on the backs of the covers of books bound in leather. The second and third divisions of this apartment are occupied by a room in which gilding and other finishing processes are performed. We observe a number of small furnaces on the table. In these the irons for gilding are heated. The fire is made by flames of gas.

This brings us to the upper story, which is the great composing-room of the establishment—that is, the room where the types are set, as will be hereafter explained. The electrotyping operations are also performed here.

Having thus given a general view of the arrangement of the Cliff Street building, and a summary account of the several operations performed in it, we shall now proceed to consider some of the most important of these operations in detail, beginning with composition, which is the first step in the complicated process of printing a book. We have first, however, in order that we may fully complete our general survey of the buildings themselves, to take a view of the interior of the court-yard.

CHAPTER V.

THE COURT-YARD.

THE two edifices of the Harper Establishment, fronting respectively on Cliff Street and Franklin Square, are separated from each other by a court-yard. This court-yard is about twenty-eight feet wide, and extends the whole length of the buildings. It contains, near the centre, three principal constructions: 1. The great chimney of the establishment; 2. The brick tower inclosing the circular staircase; and, 3. The hoistway, by which the various supplies of materials and books in the different stages of manufacture are conveyed up and down to the several stories, as required. Numerous iron bridges, connecting the different stories of the two buildings with the hoistway and the tower, pass across this court, and form one of the most striking features of it. A view of the whole is presented in the engraving on the opposite page.

INTERIOR OF THE COURT-YARD

The entrance to the court is by an arched passage-way leading from Cliff Street. A cart is represented in the engraving as coming in. The hoistway is the framed structure on the left, as seen in the engraving. It extends from the ground to some distance above the topmost story of the Cliff Street building. There is within it a movable platform, which rises and falls from top to bottom. This platform is worked by machinery connected with the steam-engine, which is placed in the court beyond the tower. This machinery acts upon the platform by means of a cable which passes over a pulley at the top of the hoistway. This pulley may be seen in the engraving, with a roof above it to protect it and the rope from the rain.

The platform itself is represented in the engraving as near the bottom of the hoistway, with a man standing upon it, whose business it is to raise and lower it, in conveying goods up and down. He controls the motions of it by means of levers placed within his reach on the platform. One of these levers communicates with the steam-engine; the other with a brake which encircles a friction-wheel, and, when in action, retards the descent. This mechanism can not be here fully described in its details. It is sufficient to say that, by the management of these levers, the man in charge can cause the platform to ascend or descend at will, with himself and all its burden upon it. He can make it move as fast or as slow as he pleases, and by means of a ratchet-wheel connected with the mechanism, can lock it at any moment whenever he wishes it to stop. He can place it in this manner opposite the doors leading to any of the various stories of the Cliff Street building, or to the bridges leading to the Franklin Square building. When the platform is so placed, the floor of it forms a continuous surface with the floor of the bridge or of the doorway, as the case may be, and thus the trucks containing the books or the paper, or whatever else it may be, that is to be transported up or down, can be drawn directly upon it.

The hoistway is six feet square, and as the breadth of the court is twenty-eight feet, it leaves twenty-two for the length of the bridges leading from it to the Franklin Square building. The bridges leading from the tower are not so long, the tower being situated nearer the centre of the court.

Some of the bridges are level, others are more or less inclined, owing to the different relative heights of the several stories of the two buildings.

The tower itself is ten feet in diameter outside, and eight within. It contains a spiral staircase of iron, with landings opposite the bridges leading to the several stories of the two buildings. The chimney, which is seen rising like a monument to some distance above the roof, is the only portion of the original establishment not destroyed by the fire. It presented a singular spectacle, rising above the blackened ruins which lay smouldering around.

All that part of the court-yard which lies beyond the tower is roofed over with glass. This roof is shown more distinctly in the plan on page 51. The inclosure contains the boilers of the steam-engine. The boilers are placed thus in the court-yard for the double purpose of security against fire, and to prevent any damage to the buildings themselves from an explosion.

The windows that open upon this court, as well as all the exterior windows of the buildings, are framed and sashed with iron, and are of very large size. Those of the principal floors are each six feet wide by twelve feet high. The average size of all the windows in the building is four feet by nine, and the whole number of windows is four hundred and thirty-four. Portions of each sash are made to move on pivots for ventilation.

It was thought best not to apply iron shutters to the windows opening into this court, as the communication of fire across the court, by the burning of the materials in any room of either building, to the opposite room in the other, is deemed all but impossible; and the iron shutters, if applied, would operate to prevent the breaking out of a fire from being so soon observed by the watchman, in case the accident should occur.

CHAPTER VI.

COMPOSITION.

THE printer's type, notwithstanding the wonders that it performs, and the vast influence which it exerts on the welfare and destiny of man, is in itself a very simple little thing. It is a small, short metallic bar, with the form of the letter which it is intended to print cast on one end of it. This engraving represents a type of the letter *m*, of the natural size—

TYPE OF A LETTER that is, of one of the natural sizes, for, of course, the breadth and thickness of the little bar varies according to the size of the intended letter, though the length is always the same, being made to conform to a common standard.

Besides letters, there are types for commas, periods, quotation marks, and all other characters used in printing. There are also shorter pieces of metal, which are put in between the words, where a little space is required to separate them. These are called *spaces* themselves. You see them represented in the annexed engraving.

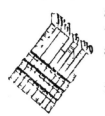

TYPES SET UP.

Of course, the forms of the letters are reversed on the types, but they come right in the printing. They come right, too, by being reflected, as you will see by holding up the page containing the preceding engraving before a mirror. When types are arranged in this way, so as to form the words that are to be printed, they are said to be *set up*, and the work of setting them up is called *composing* or *composition*.[*]

In arranging his types, the compositor has a little iron frame to set them up in, which is large enough to hold from twelve to twenty lines at a time. This instrument is called a composing-stick.

[*] The word *compose* means strictly *to place together*. In writing composition in a school, the writer arranges and puts together words and ideas to form sentences and a continued discourse, while the printer's composition is the arranging and putting together of letters to form words and sentences. So also the putting together of musical notes, in such a way as that, when they are played or sung, they will form a tune, is called *musical composition*; and, when different substances are mixed together to make a compound, the result is often termed a *composition*.

The following engraving represents the form of a composing-stick.

COMPOSING-STICK

In setting up the type in the composing-stick, the compositor stands at what is called the case. The case is a broad and shallow box, divided into a number of compartments by means of thin partitions. Each compartment is filled with the types of

THE CASE.

one particular letter or character. There are, in fact, two of these cases before each compositor. One lies directly before him, on a stand, and is placed in a sloping position, like the top of a desk. The other is farther back, and is more nearly upright. The position of both is represented in the adjoining engraving.

The first mentioned of these cases is called the *lower case*.

The other is the *upper* one. The upper case contains the capitals, small capitals, foot-note marks, dashes, &c., and the lower one the small letters, points, figures, double letters, and spaces. These, being the types most in use, are placed in the case nearest to the hand of the workman.

Below are drawers containing Italic letters, and other sorts still less frequently employed.

In respect to the compartments of the cases, there are two things particularly to be observed: one is, that they vary much in size, and the other is, that the letters are not placed in them at all in alphabetical order. Some letters occur much more frequently in our language than others. The letter e, for example, is much more common than any other; the printer consequently requires a much larger supply of e's than of the rest, and he wishes, too, to have them near at hand; whereas the letters j, and k, and x, occur very unfrequently. Quite a small compartment, therefore, will answer for them, and it may be placed, moreover, a little farther away. The case is planned, in a word, with reference to having the letters most frequently in use provided with the largest compartments, and also to having them nearest to the compositor's hand.

You can easily prove to your own satisfaction how much more numerous some letters are than others in our language, by counting the number of those of the same kind in any sentence in a book. If you take any sentence of four or five lines, you will be sure to find many more e's than any other letter, and very few j's, k's, x's, z's, and q's. You will find a considerable number of t's and a's—about three quarters as many as of the e's. Of c's you will find about *one* quarter as many, while of z's you will only find one for every sixty e's. Indeed, the proportion of the various letters in all English writing is much more regular than one would have supposed, so that it may be made quite a subject of calculation.

A very curious use of this principle is made in what is called the art of deciphering. In time of war, when letters containing orders, or any important intelligence, are sent from one officer to another, under circumstances in which it is probable that they might fall into the hands of the enemy, it is customary to write them in cipher, as it is called, that is, in secret characters; and when such letters are seized by the other party, it is a great art to decipher them. Now if the cipher, that is, the secret mode of writing, consists only of using, instead of each letter of the alphabet, some other letter or character in its place, the work of deciphering is very easy. You have only to count the number of times in which the several letters or characters occur in the writing, and the work is almost done at once. The character which has the highest number is of course e, and the others follow in almost regular order. There are a number of other curious methods and contrivances which assist in identifying the various letters and characters, that I have not time here to explain; such as if the character which stands for e comes at the end of a word of three letters several times, the other two letters are probably t and h; and also, if any word of a single letter occurs in the course of the writing, it must be either a or I, as only those letters make single words in common use in our language. By these and a few other similar principles, a number of the characters are soon ascer-

Exceptions to the general rule   How the compositor sets the type

tained, and every one that is thus ascertained helps very much to disclose the next. Indeed, this mode of writing is so easily deciphered that it is now never used; other much more difficult methods take its place.

It must not, however, be supposed, from what has been said, that the proportion of the different letters as they occur in different books is by any means entirely uniform. If a writer of a tale, for example, were to choose such a name as Zizine for the heroine of it, the compositor, in setting it up, would very soon get out of z's. Something like this, substantially, continually occurs: that is, the subject or character of a work may be such as to occasion the frequent recurrence of particular words, and this brings the letters which are contained in that word into unusual demand: so that different books *run*, as the compositors express it, upon different letters. Still, the general principle is true.

But let us return to the compositor at his case.

He does not look at the face of the type to see what letter it is when he takes it up and sets it in the composing-stick, but takes it for granted, if it comes from the right compartment, it is the right letter. He has not time to look at it more than to give it a slight glance to see that he puts it into the composing-stick right end up and right side to. He is assisted in this by what are called the *nicks* on the side of the type, which are small notches made on the side which is to be turned outward when the type is set in the composing-stick. It is much easier to set the type right by a glance at these notches, which are very conspicuous, than to look at the letter on the face of it, and see which is the top and which is the bottom of it, for this, in the case of some of the letters particularly, as, for example, the *o* and the *s*, would require very close attention.

Thus every possible arrangement is made to facilitate the work of the compositor, and enable him to get the types up as rapidly as possible from the several compartments, and to place them with the least delay in the right position in the composing-stick. By means of these facilities—that is, by having the types that are most frequently used placed nearest at hand, and having them all marked so that they may be placed in the right position at a glance—a good compositor can proceed very rapidly with his work. He has every inducement to learn to work fast, for he is paid, not by the time, but by the quantity of work which he accomplishes. The number of pages that he sets up are measured from time to time, and the amount entered on a schedule; then, at the end of the week or fortnight, he is paid according to what he has done. The unit or standard of measurement for the work is the type of the letter *m;* that type being exactly square in its form, it is easy to measure by it, for there will always be as many *ems* in a line as there are lines in a space up and down the page equal to the length of the line.

To set up a thousand ems in an hour is considered pretty good work, though some compositors will set up fifteen hundred. To do this, however, the man must be all the time on the alert, and the motions both of his eye and his hand must be very quick indeed; for we must remember that, in a thousand ems, there are

Number of types on an average in a thousand ems

many more than one thousand types to be handled, since a great many of the types, the letter *i* for example, and the comma, and the period, and the spaces, are so thin that it would take several of them to make an *m*. I learn that, upon an average, there are about three times as many types in a page as the number of ems which measure it. If this is so, a man, in order to set up a thousand ems in an hour, has to take up and place three thousand different pieces of metal. And when we consider that he has to select all these separate pieces from a great many different compartments, not less than one hundred and forty in all, some of them almost as far off from him as he can reach, and that he must place every one in just such a position in the composing-stick, and must then *justify* the line—that is, must adjust it exactly to the allotted length, it is plain that his movements must be very active to enable him to place three thousand of them in an hour.

There is a great difference in different men in respect to their natural capacity to make quick compositors. This difference does not depend altogether on their mental qualities, such as their energy, industry, and attention, but much, also, on the physical constitution of the nerves and muscles of the eye and the arm. There is a difference analogous to this in the action of certain musical instruments, such as the piano or the organ. Some respond quicker to the touch than others, on account of nice and delicate differences in the interior mechanism : that is, the connection of the series of effects, whatever they are, which intervene between the touch of the key and the production of the sound, in some instruments, is such that the process is run through with great rapidity,

Rapid compositors	Requisites.	Number of motions to be made.

and the sound follows the touch almost in an instant.   In others
it is more slow.   On instruments of the former kind, very rapid
music can be played; on the latter, only slow music, for you can
go with the succession of notes no faster than the sounds can be
produced after touching the keys; in other words, you can go no
faster than the nature of the instrument allows.   They may be
excellent instruments notwithstanding—that is, they may be excellent for the kind of music they are adapted to.   They may be
richer in tone, and more perfect in every respect than the others
except the single one of speed.

It is in some measure so with the nerves and muscles of the
arm.   When the compositor takes into his eye, from the copy
which lies before him on the upper case, any particular sentence
or word, quite a long nervous and muscular process has to be
gone through before the types representing the word find their
places in the composing-stick.   His mind first separates the word
into its letters.   His eye must then point out the several compartments, one after another, where the letters are to be found.   His
hand must move to them, and as he brings each type in toward
the stick, his eye must glance at it for an instant to catch the position of the nicks, and to direct the hand in respect to the manner
in which the type has to be turned, and then must be off again in
an instant to find the compartment which the next letter is to
come from, in order to be ready to direct the hand there the instant that the first type is placed.   Then, in turning the type
over, and bringing it in a right position into its place in the stick,
several separate motions of many different fingers are necessary,

Franklin amusing himself in his old age with composing.

each of which requires a distinct volition of the mind, and a distinct transmission of orders down the nerves of the arm. In a word, the whole process, quick as a skillful compositor is in the performance of it, is extremely complicated in its nature, and it can only be performed at the rate of over a thousand ems the hour by men whose nervous and muscular machinery is in the most perfect possible condition. There are many men who, though they may be excellently-well qualified for a hundred other things, can only make slow music in composing.

FRANKLIN.

Still, to those who perform it well, it is an easy and an agreeable occupation. The famous philosopher and statesman, Benjamin Franklin, who was a printer in early life, was accustomed, in his old age, to amuse himself with setting types and printing with his own hand, in the use of a small and convenient apparatus made expressly for the purpose.

The success of a compositor, however, does not by any means depend altogether on these physical advantages. In this, as in all other labors, they who are intent on their work, who are diligent and persevere, and who give their thoughts closely to what they are doing, and are systematic, regular, and careful, so as to make the setting right, as nearly as possible, the first time, always, in the end, win the day over the brilliant geniuses who dash on carelessly, right or wrong, and afterward lose a great deal of their time in correcting errors ; for every compositor has his own work to correct. I will now describe how this is done.

As he goes on setting up the type in the composing-stick, he places a short type at the end of every word to make the space which, on the printed page, is to separate one word from another. When he gets to the end of a line, if the work comes right, very well; if not, he makes it right by widening or narrowing the intervals between the words by means of very thin *spaces*, kept for the purpose. This process of filling out the lines is called *justifying*. It takes about a quarter as much time to justify the line as it does to pick up and place the letters of which it is composed. While justifying the line, the eye of the compositor usually runs along the line, and detects most of the errors that may have been made, and then corrects them before he proceeds. It is, of course, necessary that every line of type should fill the whole breadth of the page or column exactly, so that when the page or column is wedged up, the types of every line may be held tight in their places by the pressure of their neighbors. If the line is a broken one, as, for instance, one at the end of a paragraph, then the whole remaining space is filled up with pieces of metal similar to those placed between the words, only of much larger size. All this may be seen plainly represented in the specimen which is set up in the composing-stick on page 56. The compositor proceeds, thus setting up line after line in his compos-

| The rule | The galley | Pi | The chase |

ing-stick, until the stick is full. In order to keep the line that he is at work upon separate from the rest, and to facilitate the motion of the types in sliding into their places, he has a small tin or brass plate, called a rule, which he takes out from behind each line as soon as the line is completed, and places it above, so as to make a smooth floor, as it were, to set the new line upon. With this rule, too, he takes up the whole mass of type when the composing-stick is full, and places it away on what is called a galley.

The galley is an oblong board, with a margin about half an inch high on two sides of it, to keep the types that are placed on it from falling down. It requires great skill and dexterity, however, to handle the types when set, and to transfer them from the composing-stick to the galleys, and to move them about there, in the work of forming them into pages, and such other operations. With practice, the compositors acquire great dexterity in these manipulations, and, to the eye of the observer, they move the masses of type about as if they were so many solid blocks of metal. Sometimes, however, an accident happens; a mass of type falls upon the floor, and of course becomes a perfectly confused melange. This is called *pi*.

When the galleys are full, the *matter*, as the mass of type set up is called, is formed into pages, and placed in a frame called a *chase* to be proved. A chase is a frame of iron, divided into compartments like the sash of a window. Each compartment is intended to contain one or more pages of type, and the frame is made of iron, with strong bars crossing each other to form the compartments, in order that each page of type may be wedged in very firmly, so as to hold every type securely in its place. To do this, they place small wooden bars along the sides and ends of each page, and then drive wedges in between these bars and the iron sides of the compartment in which the page is placed. Of course the compartments of the chase are made larger than the page or pages intended to be put in them, in order to afford room for these bars and wedges. The printers call these bars *furniture;* the wedges are called *quoins*.

FORMS

The pages of type are wedged up so firmly in the chase as to form, as it were, one solid and compact mass, which can be carried from place to place with perfect safety. In former times, when it was more the custom than it is now to print directly from types, these forms had often to be carried to and fro between the composing-room and the press-room. The engraving represents Benjamin Franklin, when a journeyman printer, carrying two of them at the same time, to show the other workmen that, though he drank no strong drink, he possessed as much muscular strength as any of them.

The custom of printing from standing type is not wholly discontinued, by any means, at the present day. All newspapers, and many books, are still printed directly from the types. We often see these forms now, even in the street, as they are being conveyed from the composing-rooms, where the types have been set up and made ready, to the great printing-offices where they are to be worked on the immense presses of modern times, driven by steam. These forms, made up of the types themselves, are very massive and heavy, and there is great inconvenience in printing from them.

In order to avoid printing directly from the types, *stereotyping* was for a long time in use. This consisted in taking a mould in plaster of Paris from each page of type, and then pouring melted type-metal into the mould, thus producing a perfect cast of the surface of the page, and the printing was done from these stereotype plates. Recently, however, an improvement called *electrotyping* has been introduced.

In the Harper Establishment almost every thing at present is electrotyped. The pages of types are therefore only locked up in small chases containing one to four pages each, for the electrotyping process. The first thing is, however, to make them correct; for, notwithstanding all possible care on the part of the compositor, many of the types in every page will be found, on the first trial, to be wrong. In order to correct the errors, the form containing the page to be produced is placed upon a small hand-press, and an impression is taken. The types are inked by means

The roller for inking	Balls	Composition of the rollers

THE ROLLER

of a roller covered with ink, which the workman rolls back and forth over the pages. The form of this roller and the manner of its operation are seen in the above engraving.

The ink is taken up by the roller from a sort of table that stands near. This ink is not liquid, like writing-ink, but is thick

THE BALLS.

and viscid, like pitch; and a small quantity of it is taken up by the roller from the table, where it has been previously spread out evenly and thin, and is thence transferred to the faces of the types. In former times, balls were used for the purpose of inking the type. These balls were of the form represented in the adjoining engraving. The workman distributed the ink evenly over the balls by working and rolling the faces of them together by means of the handles attached to them, and then he would apply the ink from them to the faces of the types in the same manner. This, however, was a very laborious and slow operation, and the invention of the roller has greatly facilitated the process of inking the type. In the great

---

* These rollers are made of a composition of glue and molasses, boiled together, and then cast in iron moulds, made perfectly smooth inside. In the centre of the mould is a wooden core passing through from end to end, with iron pivots in the extremities of it, which, when the roller is finished, becomes the spindle on which it revolves.

power-presses now in general use in all the great printing establishments, there is a system of these rollers incorporated in the machinery, so that the types of the largest forms are inked without
any manual labor whatever. This will be explained more fully
by-and-by.

CHAPTER VII.

PROOFS AND CORRECTING.

THE proof, that is, the first impression from the type, made to
enable the proof-reader to examine his work, and to mark the necessary corrections, is taken, as has already been said, on a small
press, in contradistinction from the power-presses that are worked
by steam and machinery. One or more of these hand-presses
stand in the composing-room for the purpose of taking proofs.
A view of one of them is given on page 116, where it will be fully
described. The impression is taken on a small sheet—a quantity
of such sheets, previously dampened, being always ready at hand
for this purpose. The best proofs contain some errors, and most
proofs many. Words are misspelled by the accidental substitu-
tion of one letter for another; spaces are omitted: now and then a
letter is wrong side up; and perhaps a period or a note of interro-
gation, instead of taking its place properly at the end of the sentence, has intruded into the middle of a word. It would, I have
no doubt, amuse those of my readers who have never seen a proof,
if I were to insert a specimen here, with all its errors, just as they
appear when the first impression is taken; but if I were to pro-

pose to do such a thing, I presume there is not a printer in the Harper Establishment who would not be shocked at the idea of allowing any matter in such a state to go out into the world at all, on the pages of such a work as this, even as a curiosity.

When the proof has been taken, the proof-reader examines it carefully, and marks all the errors. Printers have a peculiar set of marks for the purpose of calling the attention of the compositor to the several errors, and to direct him how they are to be corrected. The compositor takes the form containing the pages of type which are to be corrected to a sort of high table, which is of a very solid and substantial construction, and there, after having loosened the pages by driving back the wedges by which they were "locked up," he proceeds to make the corrections by taking out the types that were wrong, and putting in right ones in their place. In pulling up the types that are to come out, he uses a sort of bodkin or awl, with a sharp point. This he presses against the side of the type that is to come up, and thus draws it out, and then puts the right one in its place. When the errors consist simply of wrong letters, the corrections are easily made; but if he has omitted any word, or has inserted any not found in the copy, it is more difficult to manage them. If the word to be put in is short, he can sometimes do it by taking out the spaces between the words and putting in thinner ones, thus making room for the new word. So he may sometimes take out a small superfluous word, and fill out the line by putting in thicker spaces. When there are very wide spaces between the words in any line, it is usually because the compositor has taken out a word in this way.

Reading the proof by copy   Distributing the type

But he is not allowed to make the spacing so wide as to injure the appearance of the page. If he can not get in or take out the word in this way, he has to *overrun* the matter, as it is called; that is, to carry forward one or more words from each line to the next, down to the end of the paragraph. When the corrections are all made, the pages are locked up again, and are then returned to the press, in order that a new proof may be taken.

The process of proving the work is repeated several times before it is found to be quite correct. Once it is read over carefully "by copy," as it is called, that is, by the manuscript: and finally, after it seems to be right, it is sent to the author, that he may give it a final revision. If he has made his manuscript correct in the first instance, and if the compositor and proof-reader have done their work properly, his revise will come back with very few marks upon it. The final corrections, however, which the author directs, having been made, the pages are ready to be sent to the electro-typing-room, in order that a copper fac simile of the face of it may be formed in a thin plate, for more convenient handling. When this is done, the pages of type are returned to the compositor who set them up, in order to be distributed.

The process of distributing the type—that is, of putting back the letters in the several compartments of the case where they belong, seems very surprising to those who first witness it, on account of the great rapidity with which it is performed. The compositor takes up a number of lines of type on his rule, having previously wet the whole page. This wetting causes the types to adhere together slightly, and makes it much more easy to manipulate them.

The compositor proceeds to take up several words at a time, and then, by a very dexterous motion, he throws off the several letters into their various compartments, moving his hand for this purpose with astonishing rapidity, to and fro, all about the case. A compositor will distribute five or six times faster than he can compose.

The success of the compositor, in all his work, depends very much indeed upon the correctness of his distribution; for, of course, if he has wrong type in any compartment, those type will come up when he is setting, and fill his proof with errors. It is very seldom that he sees the face of a type when he is composing; he can not stop to identify the letter in that way; he only looks at the compartment from which it comes, and at the nicks in the side of it, in order to know in what position to place it. Of course, the correctness of his composition is greatly dependent upon the correctness of his distribution.

There is a great difference in different compositors in respect to the accuracy of their work. Some proceed with so much system and care, that the whole amount of correcting which their work requires is not more than an hour or two a week. Others have to lose as much time or more every day. This, of course, is so much deducted from their earnings, since compositors are only paid for the amount of *corrected* work that they do.

Authors often unconsciously add to the labors of the compositor by inconsiderate management of various kinds, especially by making additions and alterations to their writing in the *proof*, so that, after the compositor has once set up the work, and taken a great deal of pains, by two or three corrections, to get it precisely according to the copy, and then sends a proof to the author to see if it is right, it comes back marked with numerous changes, and thus the work has all to be done, as it were, over again. It would seem, sometimes, that the author makes use of the first labors of the compositor merely to obtain a fair copy of the manuscript, in order that he may more conveniently correct and improve it. The compositor, however, receives pay for making any alterations from copy. He keeps an account of the time so employed, and charges for them. This is, of course, no more than right, as his proper business is merely to "follow copy."

There are two rules to be strictly observed by all persons who write any thing for the press:

1. Finish the writing of your book or article before you begin the printing of it. In other words, make the copy perfect, just as you wish the work to appear, before you put it into the printer's hands, so that, if possible, no alterations whatever may be required after it is once in type.

2. In preparing the copy which you intend for the compositor, write only on one side of the sheet of paper, and write in a plain, distinct, and legible hand, every word in full, and all the paragraphs, divisions, headings, and stops, and other marks, just as you wish them to appear. The compositor's rule is to conform to the copy precisely in all these particulars. Indeed, the rule which Benjamin Franklin gave to the journeymen in his office, and which is, in some sense, the rule of all good compositors to the present day, was, Follow your copy, if you follow it out of the window.

It unfortunately happens that some authors are so careless with their manuscripts, that, in following this rule when setting up for them, the poor compositor gets sent, as it were, out of the window very often.

CHAPTER VIII.
TYPE-FOUNDING.

I HAD often heard that the making of types was an exceedingly ingenious and curious process, and when I had finished the foregoing description of the manner in which these little wonder-workers are set up, it occurred to my mind that it would be a good plan for me to visit one of the principal foundries in New York, and see for myself how the work of manufacturing them was performed. I accordingly called upon the Messrs. Harper, and asked one of the gentlemen for the address of one of the foundries from which they obtained their supplies. He accordingly gave me the address, and I immediately proceeded to the type-founding establishment. One of the proprietors received me very kindly, and conducted me through the rooms to witness the different processes.

"In former times," said he, as we walked together up stairs in going to the upper stories of the building, where the various operations of the manufactory were carried on, "in former times, it was customary to cast types in little moulds held in the hand, the melted metal being poured in from a small ladle, but now they are made far more rapidly by means of a machine."

He also explained to me the composition and the properties of the metal used for the casting. It seems that it must possess the following properties: It must be *hard*, but not too *brittle*. It must also be easily fused, and not subject to rust.

It must be hard; for, if it were soft, like lead, the face of the type would not stand under the great pressure required in printing, and the edges of the letter, too, would be battered and bruised from the little knocks which the types necessarily get from each other in the processes of being set up and distributed.

For a similar reason, it must not be brittle, for then the edges would break and crumble.

It must be easily fusible. Iron, for example, does not melt at less than a red heat, and it would be extremely difficult, if not impossible, to manage such small castings at so great a temperature.

It must be a metal, too, not subject to rust; for, in using the types, it is often necessary to wet them, and thus, if they were made of any easily oxydizable metal, they would soon become rusted and spoiled.* For this reason, therefore, as well as for the other, iron would not answer for types.

In fact, there is no one simple metal that is suitable. There is some good and valid objection to every one. The type-makers have, however, discovered a compound of three metals which answers the purpose very well. The three metals are lead, tin, and

* When iron rusts, the metal combines at the surface with one of the components of water, called *oxygen* This compound of iron and oxygen forms the brown powder which we call *rust*. Lead, when thus combined with oxygen, forms a *white* powder, and sometimes a *red* powder. But lead will not combine with the oxygen by simple exposure to the atmosphere, or contact with water, as iron will. Lead, therefore, is said not to be easily oxydizable

antimony. Neither of them by itself would make a good type, but, combined together in certain proportions, they form just the material that is required. The compound melts easily, and it becomes hard, but not brittle, when cold. Then there is another point which is of great importance, namely, that it does not shrink much in cooling. If the metal were to shrink in cooling, then the face of the type would lose its fullness and sharpness of form, and thus become more or less imperfect and irregular.

While the proprietor of the foundry was explaining these things to me on the way up stairs, he stopped at a little office in one of the rooms to show me some specimens of type metal. He cut some of these with a knife, to let me see how hard and tough the metal was. It seemed to be harder than lead, but not nearly so hard as copper.

Soon after this we entered the casting-room, which was in the upper story of the building. There was a range of workmen all around the room, each busy casting type at his little machine. The machines had each its own separate furnace and reservoir of metal, so that they looked like so many little forges ranged in order all about the room.

We walked up toward one of the machines that stood near a window, to witness the operation of it. I was greatly astonished at the spectacle. I have seen very ingenious mechanical contrivances before—those for making pins, for example—where a coil of wire is drawn in at one end of the machine, and pins drop out of the other almost as fast as you can count them. But this seemed more surprising still, for it was a mass of hot, melted metal, bub-

CASTING.

bling and simmering, as it were, over its little furnace that supplied the material. By the simple turning of a crank on the part of the operator, as a boy would turn a small grindstone or a coffee-mill, this melted metal was taken up, a little at a time, at the upper part of the machine, and dropped out in types below, cool and solid.

But I must describe the machine a little more particularly. It appeared to be complicated in its construction, but the principle of its operation, as is usually the case, indeed, with all great inventions, was very simple. The essential thing is a mould to cast the types in, made in parts, so as to open for the purpose of letting the type drop out, and then to shut up together again very closely and exactly. The several parts forming the mould are so connected with machinery worked by the crank that they are opened and shut again every time the crank is turned once round.

Besides this action of opening and shutting the mould, with all the complicated mechanism which is connected with it, it has an-other movement. Every time the crank revolves, it is brought up to what might be called the mouth of the furnace, to receive the supply of melted metal, and then is brought away again. This mouth is very small, the orifice not being much larger, perhaps, than a large pin-hole. At the instant the mouth of the mould is brought up in contact with 'this little opening by the moving of the crank, a jet of melted metal, just enough to fill the mould, is forced in by means of a small force-pump in the reservoir. This force-pump is worked by the same crank which gives motion to the mould. In a word, the machine is so contrived that the oper-ator, by simply turning this crank, brings up the mould to the furnace, pumps in enough of metal for the casting of one type, withdraws the mould, opens it to let the type drop out, and then puts the mould together again for a fresh operation.

The types, though cool enough to be solid when they drop, are still very hot. They are caught, therefore, as they fall, upon a little paper apron under the machine, and thence, cooling as they go, they are gradually shaken down by the types that continue to fall upon the apron from above, and finally descend into a box placed a little below to receive them.

The operation was performed with astonishing rapidity. I took out my watch while standing near one of the fastest of the ma-chines, in order to see how rapidly the types were produced by it. I found that thirty-six types were dropped in a quarter of a min-ute, or over eight thousand in an hour. It is true that this ma-chine was casting small type, and that it worked faster than most others in the room. The average, however, could not have been less than two thousand in an hour.

It is by no means to be supposed, however, that because the operation of the machine thus described seems so simple, the artisan who works it has nothing to do but to turn a crank. This is, indeed, all the mechanical work that he has to perform, but in the exercise of judgment, skill, and discretion, he has a great deal to do. He must watch his furnace and his reservoir of melted metal, to see that the metal is always of the proper temperature. He must be careful, too, that he does not turn the machine too fast, for this would heat the mould too much, and thus prevent the perfect form of the type. He must continually keep his eye on the little orifice where the metal is ejected from the reservoir, to see that all is right there, and that no little globules of melted metal remain on the outside of it to prevent a perfect junction of the face of the mould with the outside surface. In a word, a person, to be a good type-founder, notwithstanding all the help he obtains from his machine, must be a man of great skill, careful judgment, and practical dexterity.

The metal, in being injected or forced into the mould, passes through an opening, which forms a sort of long, slender funnel,

which enters at the lower end of the mould. This funnel itself, as well as the mould, becomes filled with metal, so that, when the type drops upon the paper below this metal remains attached to it in the form of a long and slender wedge-shaped projection called a *jet*, which is represented in the adjoining engraving. This jet

THE JET

must, of course, be removed in the process of finishing the type.
Indeed, the removing of it is the first step in the finishing process.

They *break* it off.   It breaks very easily, being quite slender
at the point of its junction with the type.   One would not suppose
that there would be any thing particularly curious or interesting
in so simple an operation as this, but I found it quite curious,
on account of the great rapidity with which the boys, whose business it is, perform it, and the arrangements which were made to
facilitate the work.   The process is called breaking, and the boys
who do it are called *breakers*.

The breaker is seated, when at work, at a sort of low table, with
sides all around it, to prevent the types from falling upon the floor.
The centre of the table directly before him is covered with a sort
of cushion, or, rather, as perhaps I ought to say, the bottom of the
box which the table forms is lined with a sort of cushion covered
with smooth leather.   At one end of the table, within the box, is
a great pile of types, with the jets attached to them, just as they
come from the moulds.   These the boy continually draws down
upon the surface of the cushion, where he breaks off the jets from
them with an inconceivably rapid motion of the fingers, and then
separates the parts by pushing the jets one way and the types
another.   The boy whom I watched performed the operation so
rapidly that, with the closest observation, I could not follow the
motions of his fingers at all, or see by what means he contrived to
accomplish the object.

Of course, at the point where the jet was broken off, the mark
of the fracture would remain at the end of the type, producing a

sort of blemish. It was curious to see how simply and easily this mark was afterward removed. A long row of the types were set up together, side by side, in a long and slender frame, and then a little plane, the rim of which came almost to a point, and was ground at the end to the form of an exceedingly small gouge, was passed along the whole line, and thus, by a single stroke of the tool, the fractured portion was cut out from the ends of hundreds of types at a time.

The next process to breaking was what was called rubbing. The rubbing was the work of women and girls. The room where this operation was performed had two or three long low tables extending through it from end to end, with what seemed to be a row of grindstones lying upon them. These stones were large and not very thick, and they were lying on their sides upon the tables. The upper surface of them seemed to be very level and flat, and were of about the roughness of sand-paper. Before each stone sat a female operative rubbing types. The object of this rubbing was to smooth the sides of the type, and to remove a little thin projection of metal which is apt to be left, after the casting, at the edges. This projection is caused by the protrusion of the metal a little way into the joints of the mould; for the mould, you will recollect, is made of several distinct parts, which open after the casting, to allow the type to drop out, and then shut together again. Now it is not possible to make these joints perfectly tight, I suppose. Indeed, it is necessary to allow sufficient opening to permit the escape of the air, for the metal can not enter the mould any faster than the air which was previously in it can go out. Now

10 F

Account of the process of *rubbing*	Setting	Types placed in rows

the metal itself, at the moment of casting, will protrude a little way into these interstices, and to remove the protrusions thus formed is one object of the rubbing.

The girl takes up a handful of types, and lays them down, side by side, on the stone. She takes ten or twenty at a time. She then lays two of her fingers across the types, and, by a sweep of her arm to and fro, she rubs them back and forth on the flat surface of the stone. This smooths and evens the under sides of the types. Then she brings the types to the edge of the stone, so as to allow the ends of the whole row to project a little, and by a very dexterous movement—so dexterous and quick, indeed, that you will have to look very closely to follow it—she turns them all over together, and then proceeds to rub the other side, and finally pushes them into a box ready near the stone to receive them.

After a time, the stones, I was told, become glazed over, as it were, by the rubbing of the types upon them, and then it becomes necessary to restore the roughness of the surface before they can be used any more. This is done by grinding them with sand.

The next process is *setting*. This consists of the work of arranging the types in rows for inspection and for the final finishing. The setters are usually small girls. The types are taken up by them from a box, where they lie in bulk, and are placed in a row upon a long stick, like a yard-stick. It is astonishing to witness the rapidity of motion and the accuracy which these girls display in taking up and placing the types, arranging them all the same way, that is, with the same side toward them, and the letter faces all turned downward. In the first instance, the girls set the types

Picture of the *dresser* examining the types with a magnifying-glass.

in a shorter stick, much like a composing-stick in respect to the manner in which it is used, only it is eight or ten inches long, and just wide enough for one row of types. As fast as this stick becomes full, the girls transfer the row of types to the long stick, which lies on a little shelf before them, and when this is full the whole line is made ready to be passed into the hands of the dresser.

THE DRESSER.

This brings us to the next operation, which is that of *dressing* the type. The dresser carefully examines them, and rejects those that are imperfect and bad, and then trims those that are perfect to an exact and a uniform standard. The casting, to be sure, leaves them nearly uniform, but not quite. It is the last finishing touch to form the types which the dresser gives to them. For this object, he arranges them on an instrument which has the appearance of a very long rule. There is a ledge below for the foot of the types to stand upon, and a sort of chock at each end, one of which is movable, and works by a screw. By means of these, the types, when necessary, may be all clamped together. The dresser arranges his types in a line on this rule, and places them in a strong light at a table opposite the window. They stand there before him in a strong and glittering row, like a long line of soldiers waiting for inspection. Holding a little awl or bodkin in his right hand, and in his left, close to his eye, a small magnifying-glass, he passes his glass along the line, looking closely at the face of every type. All that are perfect he passes; but, whenever he sees any little blemish or imperfection on the surface of the metal which forms the face of the letter, he instantly pulls the type forward out from among its fellows with his bodkin, and it drops, condemned and disgraced, into an apron placed below to receive it, whence it is sent back in due time to the melting-pot, to try its chance again. As near as I could judge, something like one tenth of the types were thus condemned.

The types that pass inspection are then screwed up together to receive their final trimming, the dresser maneuvering and manipulating them for this purpose with surprising dexterity, causing them to change front, face about, and turn, now this side toward him and now that, all together, with an adroitness that would astonish the most skillful general that ever maneuvered soldiers on parade.

It is in the course of this process of dressing that the workman planes out the mark of the fracture left at the foot of the type by breaking off the jet, as has before been explained.

When the dressing process has been completed, the types are finished. They are then set up together solid, in square blocks of about the size of one of these pages, those of the same letter or character together. These blocks are then carefully enveloped and packed, and are ready for sale.

The quantity of metal thus cast into types at the establishment that I visited amounts to not less than 500,000 pounds every year, and nearly two hundred hands are constantly employed in the various processes. This fact alone shows on how magnificent a scale the printing operations of the present day are conducted. One of the results of the progress which the printing art has thus made is, that more copies of the Bible are now printed in two years than the whole number that had ever been printed before the commencement of the present century since the art of printing was discovered.

It is very probable that in respect to the printing of books and newspapers the advance has been greater still.

CHAPTER IX.

MOULDS FOR TYPE-FOUNDING.

THE process of forming the types themselves from the melted metal, nice and curious as it is, is by no means the most delicate and difficult part of the type-founder's work. The great thing is the making of the mould, or, rather, of that part of the mould by which the face of the letter is formed. The part in question is called the *matrice*, because it is the mother, as it were, of all the

Picture of a matrice	Description of it	The punches

THE MATRICE

types that are cast in it. The matrice is a short and thick bar or block of copper, with the form of the letter which it is intended to produce from it stamped in one of the four sides of it, near the end. It is about as long as a type, but a great deal broader and thicker. Of course, there must be a separate matrice for every separate letter or character. The matrices are all of the same length, and are so made that any of them that belong to the same set can be inserted into any mould, though the letters and characters which are stamped upon them are of course different in each different matrice.

In every machine or mould for casting type there is a place for inserting the matrice, and the founder can put in any one he pleases, according to the type or character which he wishes to cast. The matrice is so placed in the mould that the part on which the letter is stamped comes exactly opposite the head of the type, and thus the metal, at the moment of casting, flows into the stamped depression, and forms the letter that is stamped upon the matrice, whatever it may be.

Thus we see very easily how the letters are formed on the types by means of the impression in the matrice, but now the question arises how the impressions in the matrices are made. The answer is, that they are stamped in the copper by means of what are called *punches*. By examining the engraving on the following page, the reader will be able to form a pretty correct opinion of how punches are made.

THE PUNCHES.

The punch consists of a small steel rod, with a letter cut upon one end, and a flat head, to receive the blow of a hammer, at the other. The punches are about two or three inches long, and are made of the best and hardest steel. The letter is cut upon them by hand, in the use of chisels, files, and other such instruments; and as the form and fashion of all the impressions in the matrices, and of all the castings on the types, and of all the letters in the printed books which may come from them, depend upon their shape and finish, the utmost possible pains is taken in perfecting them.

The letters are formed in the matrice by means of the punch, the letter end of it being driven into the copper by the blow of a hammer. A man who owns a set of punches often sells a set of impressions from them to a type-founder, to save the founder the expense of making the punches himself. He calls it selling *drives*.

Thus, in coming to the punches, we come at last to the point where the form of the letter has its actual origin. It begins with the punch, the punch makes the matrice, the matrice makes the type, and the type makes the electrotype, and the electrotype makes the letter on the printed page. Thus every letter which you see in this book has come to you through all these five different forms.

This seems, at first view, to be taking a great deal of trouble; but, on reflection, we shall see that the process is admirably calculated to save labor and trouble. If, for example, every type were formed by itself, by cutting out the letter upon the end of it with chisels and files, instead of casting it in a matrice, the work of forming them would be pretty much the same as that of making the punches—a day's labor nearly to each one; whereas now they are cast, as we have seen, at the rate of from two thousand to eight thousand in an hour. So in respect to the matrices. To form a matrice by means of cutting-tools would be even more laborious and troublesome than the making of a punch, and there would be only one matrice when it was done. But the punch, once finished, is the means of making hundreds of matrices, each being formed at a blow.

The effect of the whole system in respect to the multiplication of results is amazing, as will be readily seen by the following calculation: One punch will make from fifty to one hundred matrices. These matrices, distributed in the various machines of many different founders, will cast each many millions of types, making many hundreds of millions of types from one punch. Each of these types used in electrotyping will give from five hundred to one thousand electrotype copies, and every electrotype used in printing will give a million of impressions on a printed page. This makes an aggregate of many *thousands of millions of millions* of printed letters from one single father punch, the common progenitor of all. This is no imaginary or fanciful calculation. It is a fair and honest statement of the actual powers of the system as now in constant operation, and it is in consequence of this enormous multiplication of results that the art of printing is enabled to perform such wonders, and to exert such an influence as it does on the destinies of man.

Of course, a punch that is to exert so wide-spread an influence in the world well deserves that no pains or expense should be spared in giving it, at the outset, the most perfect possible form. Consequently, the cutting and the polishing of the punches is one of the most delicate and important of all the processes connected with the typographical art. The punches are, consequently, very costly, and a good set of them is highly prized. A very large number, too, are required in every extensive foundry. One might at first suppose that a few hundred would be enough, as there are only twenty-four letters in the alphabet, and a comparatively small number of stops and marks besides. But, instead of a few hundreds, many thousands are required. In the first place, there must be two sets of capitals, and one set each for Roman and Italic letters, and one set for figures, for every size of type. These, with the necessary stops and other characters, make at least three hundred punches for every size. Then the number of sizes and styles of letters in ordinary use is very large, so that there is scarcely any limit to the number and variety of punches that are required. They amounted, in the establishment that I was visiting, to many thousands, and the value of them was from thirty to forty thousand dollars. The value of the matrices, too, was about the same.

I went to see the iron safes where this valuable property was deposited. These safes—which are the same with those customarily used by the New York merchants for keeping their account-

books and other valuables from thieves and fire—are great iron
chests, made movable on monstrous castors, with walls eight or
ten inches thick all around.   These walls are formed inside and
out of thick plates of iron, bolted together in the most substantial
manner, and filled in with a mineral composition peculiarly adapted to resist the action of fire.   The doors are of the same construction as the walls, and they move, of course, very slowly and
heavily on their massive hinges.

The first safe that I visited contained punches, and the whole
interior of it was filled with a system of small shallow drawers,
each of which contained a number of round tin boxes, in which
the punches were packed, those of the same size in the same box.
They were packed in an upright position, with the letters on the
upper end of them.

I afterward went to see the safes that contained the matrices.
There were two of these safes, and they were much larger than the
one which I had first visited, for the matrices are far more numerous than the punches.   These safes, too, were filled with little
drawers, all of which were appropriately numbered and labeled according to the denomination, style, and character of the letters
which the matrices that they contained were intended to make.
The contents of these safes were of very great value.   In addition
to the usual securities for the protection of them in case of fire,
they were banded very strongly with thick bars of iron, made to
close over the doors after they were shut, and to lock independ-
ently of them.   The object of these bands was to assist in pre-
venting the safe from bursting open when falling through the floors

of the building into the cellar in case of a fire: for always, when a building is burned that contains safes of this character in the upper stories, the safes, as soon as the timbers of the floor on which they stand are weakened by the fire, break through, and fall with a dreadful crash down through all the other floors into the cellar. Indeed, so great is the force of the fall of these safes sometimes, that they bring down the walls of the building with them, the ends of the floor-timbers being built into the walls in such a manner that when the timbers are broken off and borne down in the inside, the walls are pried over as by a lever, and come down with a dreadful crash and confusion into the street, overwhelming and burying the firemen, perhaps, in the ruin.

The safes of a type-foundry are peculiarly heavy, being filled, not with books and accounts, or other comparatively light articles, but with pieces of metal, which, though individually small, are so numerous, and so closely packed, that the whole safe, in respect to its heaviness, is very much as if it were one solid mass of iron six feet square and three feet deep. Of course, so ponderous a body as this, in falling fifty or sixty feet through the floors of a burning building, must come down to the cellar floor with a tremendous concussion, and there would be most imminent danger that it would burst itself open, unless its fastenings were secured in the strongest possible manner.

Indeed, the whole building used for the purposes of a type-foundry must be made extremely strong, on account of the great weight which almost every part of it has to carry. The packages of types, of course, as arranged on the shelves of the store-room, ready to be boxed for their various destinations, are as heavy almost as so many blocks of solid metal. I saw one set of very strong and massive shelves, perhaps ten feet wide, and ten feet high in all, which contained packages of type that weighed, in all, I was informed, not less than ten tons. The whole solid stock of type on hand in the establishment weighed usually not less than forty or fifty tons.

In fitting up the types for use, those of each letter are put together in a package by itself, so that one package, when opened, is found to be all a's, another all b's, and so on. The reader might perhaps suppose, at first thought, that the number of types for each letter of the alphabet would be equal. But this is by no means the case, for some letters occur much more frequently than others, and, of course, more types of them are required in proportion than of the others.

For example, almost twice as many are required of the letter e as of any other letter, for the e occurs twice as frequently as any other letter of the alphabet in the English language. This subject has already been referred to in describing the setting of type. Next to the letter e, the letters a, n, and o are most common. For every seven pounds of e's they usually put about four pounds of a's, n's, and o's ; that is, a little more than one half as many. The most unfrequent letters are q, x, and z. Of each of these only one quarter of a pound are required for every seven pounds of e's, which is in the proportion of one to twenty-eight.

It is surprising what a variety of effects can be produced by type made in this way, from matrices formed by punches of steel.

There is a style of type in which the letters seem to touch each other on the printed page, and form what appears to be a continuous writing.

Mrs A accepts with pleasure Mrs B's kind invitation for Thursday, Monday morning

This is called script type. It looks quite continuous, like real writing; but if you examine it very closely, especially with a microscope, you will see a slight division in the hair-line which unites each letter with the one that precedes and follows it. These divisions denote the points of junction between the several types as they stand in the line.

A great many different styles of ornamental borders are made in the same way, that is, by means of separate types, the figure on each of which is carried out so close to the edge of it as to come almost into absolute contact with the corresponding parts of the figure on the next type. Thus, in the printing, the effect of a continuous border is produced. Type-founders invent an infinite variety of these borders, each differing from the rest in style and design. On the next page is a small specimen of one of them.

These borders are used to form ornamental margins for cards, certificates, catalogues, and other similar publications, and sometimes, too, for the pages of printed books. I insert a specimen

Further specimens of what can be done by means of punches

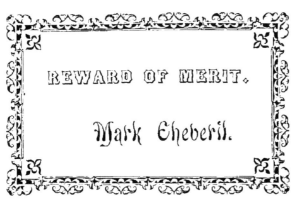

here to show how great is the variety of work accomplished by the punch, and how nice must be the skill of the cutter to work such fine and complicated designs in the solid metal. Many of these borders are very large and exceedingly elaborate. Others are small and very delicate in style of execution, and by varying the combinations of them a great variety of effects may be produced. In the margin is a small circle formed by arranging together the four corner types of a particular border, with a specimen of fine printing within it, which shows to how great a degree of minuteness the work of cutting the punches is sometimes carried.

And here I will close the account of this curious manufacture, only adding that the types made where the English language is spoken are by no means restricted to the English language in speaking themselves. They can talk in any language in which the alphabetic characters are the same as in our own. Thus the progeny of the same punch, formed by an American workman in New York, are scattered in innumerable thousands over the world.

They talk Spanish in Mexico, Portuguese in Brazil, and French in New Orleans or Montreal. They are employed, too, in every variety of duty. Some, in spelling-books or primers, are set to the work of teaching millions of little children in schools to read and spell. Others, that came out, perhaps, originally side by side with the former from the same matrice, are employed in Latin dictionaries, or in new and beautiful editions of the ancient classics, to aid the learned researches of scholars in colleges and universities. Some amuse in books of romance. Others, the brothers and sisters of the former, puzzle and perplex in books of mathematics. Some go to Washington, and make fierce political speeches, now in favor of one party, and now in favor of the other, equally indifferent to both; others to a Bible House or a Tract House, and earnestly plead the cause of human salvation; while others still devote their lives to the fireside entertainment and instruction of thousands of families through the pages of story-books or magazines. All this time the parent punch from whom they all sprung remains wholly unconscious of the immense diffusion of his offspring, and of the vastly varied character of the duties which they are severally called upon to fulfill. He pays no heed to these incalculable results of what he has already done, and least of all does he show any disposition to be satisfied with them. His duty is to go on producing; so he holds well to his temper and to his edge, and keeps steadily on, adding continually, through the new matrices that he produces, millions and millions more to his already innumerable progeny.

CHAPTER X.

ELECTROTYPING.

THE electrotyping process is one which has been discovered within a very few years, and it very greatly facilitates all printing operations which are carried on upon an extensive scale. It consists in producing from the solid page of types, or of types and engraved blocks together—which, of course, is very heavy and unwieldy—a plate of copper, with all the faces of the letters and the lines of the engravings precisely repeated on the side of it, just as they appear in the solid page which the compositor had set up. The original page of the types can then be sent back to the composing-room and distributed, and the new and comparatively light, thin copper plate can be used to print from in its stead.

The electrotype plate is about three sixteenths of an inch in thickness. In length and breadth, of course, it corresponds with the size of the page that it was made from. The face of it is of copper; the back of it, including the principal portion of its thickness, is of type-metal.

When it is to be used in printing, it is placed upon a block of wood of such a thickness that the block and the plate together shall equal the thickness of the original page of type. The block is provided with a pair of clamps to secure the plate in its place. The upper ends of these clamps are seen in the engraving, on the edge of the block that is toward us, projecting over the edge of the plate, which is beveled to receive them. The back edge of the plate is also beveled, and passes under two fixtures projecting on that side, which are attached firmly to the block. The clamps on the hither side are movable, being made so that they can be drawn back or driven forward by means of the toothed wheels, which are seen near the back edge of the block. These wheels are each con-

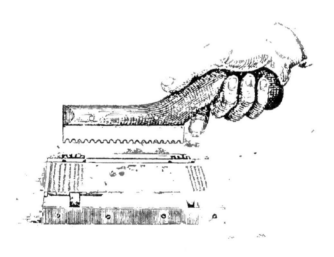

BLOCKING THE PLATE.

structed with a brass rod, which serves as an axle, and communicates with the clamps on the front side of the plate. The rods are connected with these clamps by a screw, so that, by turning the toothed wheels, the clamps may be drawn in over the edge of the plate, and thus made to hold it down securely on the face of the block. The other side of the plate is held down, of course, by the beveled edge being brought close under the fixed clamps on that side.

The instrument with which the toothed wheels are worked, both in fastening in the plate and loosening it again when required, is seen above, as held when in use by the workman.

The plate, as will be seen by the engraving, is quite thin. It shows on the upper surface a map, occupying the centre of the page, with a few lines of letter-press above and below. Of course, in forming this page, the wooden block on which the map was engraved was placed in the centre, and the lines of type, after being set up in the composing-stick, were placed at each end. The whole page was then wedged up in a chase, and sent to the electrotyper.

The upper surface of the electrotype only—that is, the one which contains the forms of the letters and the lines of the engraving, is of copper. The remainder of the thickness of it, as has already been said, is of type-metal, which is cast upon the back of the thin copper plate, to stiffen and support it. The chief interest in respect to the electrotyping process is the manner in which this thin copper plate is made.

A visitor going into a room where the electrotyping process is going on, sees little else but a large number of square boxes or tanks, filled with some chemical-looking liquor, and connected together by means of a great number of bent and crooked wires, which run in irregular curves from one tank to another. These wires are for the purpose of carrying an electric current to the liquor in the tanks. The current is supplied from what is called a galvanic battery, which also stands in the room.

To describe the construction and uses of a galvanic battery would lead me too far away from the subject of printing. It will be sufficient for my present purpose to say, that a current of electricity from such a battery, directed upon the liquor in the tank, is essential to the success of the electrotyping process, and, accordingly, the battery and wires are arranged for the purpose of supplying such a current. The general principle on which the process is conducted is this.

It has been discovered within a few years that if a liquid contains any metal in solution, an arrangement may be made of electric wires, so that, under the influence of the electric current brought by the wires, the particles of the metal in the solution will be slowly deposited upon any metallic plate which may be immersed in the liquid, although no such effect would be produced without the electric current. For example, if a liquid containing copper in solution were to be placed in a tank, and a silver dollar were to be immersed in it, no effect would be produced.* If, now, a galvanic battery be established near the place, to supply a current of electricity, and wires are placed in a peculiar way, connecting the battery with the liquor in the tank, and also with the silver dollar, the copper will begin immediately to leave the liquor, and to deposit itself in a thin film all over the surface of the silver, and will soon encase it entirely. This process will go on as long

---

* Copper itself, in its metallic state, can not be dissolved in water, but some of its compounds with other substances can be. For example, *blue vitriol*, which is a compound of sulphuric acid and copper, is easily soluble. Of course, in a solution of *blue vitriol* in water, we should have the particles of copper diffused throughout the liquid, though in a wholly invisible form.

as the current of electricity continues, and the supply of copper in the solution holds out. Thus a copper covering of any required thickness may be applied to the silver.

The process of electrotyping is conducted on this principle. A thin film of copper is deposited in the manner above described upon a mould which contains a perfect impression of the whole page which is to be cast, both type-matter and engravings. The mould is formed from the page as it is set up in the composing-room by pressing the face of it into a certain plastic substance prepared for the purpose. When the mould is thus formed, and the surface of it is prepared properly for receiving the metallic deposit, it is placed in one of the tanks, and then connected with the battery by the wires. The deposition of the copper all over the surface of the mould immediately commences. The particles find their way into all the interstices of the type, and into the very finest lines of the engraving, so as to reproduce exactly every touch and lineament, however delicate and fine, of the engraved work.

After the process has been continued several hours, until the workman considers that the coating of copper is sufficiently thick to sustain itself under the subsequent operations, he takes the mould out, and the copper coating is detached from it. The plate is exceedingly slender and thin when first detached, but all the letters of the types, and all the lines, and even the very finest shades of the engraving, are represented upon it with beautiful distinctness and precision. The impression is, of course, in relief on one side, and in intaglio on the other. This thin plate is then placed on a sort of frame, with supports to keep it extended in a true and

INTERIOR OF THE VAULTS.

even position, and a backing of type-metal is cast upon what a lady would call the *wrong side* of it, and thus a solid, substantial plate is formed, thick and firm enough to be used safely in printing, and yet not one fifth part as heavy as the original page of type-matter from which it was formed.

The plates are all minutely examined when they are cast, and are properly trimmed and finished. They are made as nearly as possible of a uniform thickness. Of course, there must be one plate for every page of the book to be printed.

The accumulation of electrotype plates in a large establishment that has been long in operation is very great. In the Harper Establishment, the stores now on hand are enormous. Those of the Magazine alone are rapidly approaching ten thousand.

The plates are stored in subterranean vaults built under the streets that surround the building. The entrance to these vaults has already been shown in the sectional view of the Cliff Street building, on page 42. A more enlarged view is shown on the preceding page. The vaults extend under ground for two hundred feet in length, and in dimensions are eight feet wide by eight feet high. They are shelved on both sides, and the shelves are loaded with plates—stereotype or electrotype—representing all the works published in the establishment. There is one plate for every page of every one of the many hundreds of volumes which the house publishes, making from fifty to seventy tons in all.

When a new edition of any book is required, the plates are brought out from these vaults and put upon the presses. When the work is finished, they are taken back again to the vaults.

CHAPTER XI.

ENGRAVINGS.

To those who have not had an opportunity to know much about the processes of printing, there is quite a mystery in respect to the manner in which the engravings are made.

There are two entirely distinct modes of making and printing engravings in common use. These two modes are usually distinguished as *copper-plate* or *steel* engravings, and *wood* engravings.*

The former kind—that is, the copper-plate engravings, were made by cutting the lines of the picture in the surface of the copper-plate, and then filling these lines with ink, and afterward taking up the ink upon the sheet of paper by a strong pressure.

The second kind—that is, the wood engravings, were made by drawing the figure on the end of a block of very hard and close-grained wood, previously made smooth for the purpose, and then cutting away the wood from between the lines of the drawing, so as to leave the lines themselves in relief, thus exactly reversing the process in copper-plate engraving, in which the lines themselves were cut away. The figure was then transferred to the paper by inking the faces of the lines, and printing from them in a common printing-press, precisely as from types.

* Besides these, there is a third class of illustrations much in use, called lithographs They are, however, not properly engravings, being printed from simple *drawings* made upon stone, and, therefore, they are not included here

The names copper-plate engraving and wood engraving are, however, no longer strictly appropriate; for, instead of plates of copper, plates of *steel* are now generally used for the former mode. The steel is softened in the first instance, so as to facilitate the cutting of the lines upon it, and then is afterward hardened again, so as to make it more enduring under the constant rubbing to which it is subjected in the process of printing. It is wholly on account of its being so much more enduring than copper that steel is now more generally used for the material of the plate on which this class of engravings are made.

The essential distinction between the two modes is that, by the former, the lines of the design are cut in *intaglio*, as it is called, while by the latter they stand in relief.

Copper or steel engraving has this advantage over wood, namely, that finer work may be executed in that way. This, we might easily see, must necessarily be the case, since, in engraving a fine design, it must be much more easy to cut the lines themselves in the material of the surface to be engraved, than to cut away the material on each side of the line, so as to leave the line itself in relief. It is subject to this great disadvantage, however, namely, that it requires an entirely different mode of printing from the ordinary letter-press of books—one, moreover, that is very laborious and slow; for, in the first place, the whole surface of the plate is covered with ink by means of a roller. The plate is then carefully wiped, so as to remove all the ink from the surface, and leave only that which lies in the lines of the engraving. The ink, lying as it does beneath the surface of the plate in the engraved lines,

Mode of printing from copper and steel engravings.

must be *brought up*, as it were, by the impression: and this requires a very great force. This force is applied by passing the plate, with the sheet on which the impression is to be taken, under a roller. By this means, the whole force of the pressure is

COPPER-PLATE PRINTING.

brought upon the different portions of the sheet in succession, at the line of contact with the roller, instead of being diffused over the whole surface, and thus, in a great degree, weakened. The adjoining engraving represents the general form of one of these printing-presses as used fifty years ago. Great improvements have been made in the construction of these presses since those days, but the principle is the same at the present day.

In printing from wood engravings, on the other hand, or from electro-plates, which are fac similes of them in copper, the lines of the design are *in relief*, precisely like the faces of the types; and the ink may be taken off from them by the same general pressure, exerted simultaneously over the whole surface of the plate, as that which takes the impression from the types. This species of engraving can consequently be worked in the same page with letter-press, and by the same impression.

This difference is of immense importance in respect to the practical working of the two methods, where great numbers of impressions are required. The engravings for Harper's Magazine, for example, by being cut in relief, can be worked in the power-presses with the other matter of the number. By this means, they can be printed with great rapidity, although still, on account of the vast number of copies that are required, the operation occupies a considerable time. If, however, the engravings were all in one form, the whole hundred and forty thousand copies could be worked off in a little more than a month from one press.*

If, now, on the other hand, we suppose the engravings to be executed in steel or copper, the result would be astonishingly different. I find, by an examination of the last number of the Magazine that has been issued at the present time, that it contains not less than sixteen solid pages of engravings. If we suppose that two of these pages were engraved on one plate, it would require, at the usual rate of printing by this method—say two hundred and fifty impressions per day—not much less than *two years* to work off the necessary number of copies from *one plate*, and that would be only two pages out of the sixteen; so that it would take *twelve or fifteen years*, with one copper-plate press, to print all the engravings required for one number, instead of a month or thereabout, as by the present method. Of course, by multiplying the

* In point of fact, the engravings are scattered through many forms, and it takes several presses, therefore, to print the engravings of one number within the month, and as portions of several numbers are being printed at the same time, there is an average of ten or twelve presses constantly employed on the Magazine. Sometimes twenty are at work upon it at one time.

presses used, the work would be hastened, but it would require many hundreds of presses to do the work of one number within the month.

Thus we see that steel and copper-plate engravings can only be used as illustrations of literary works in cases where the number of copies to be issued is comparatively small. Then, moreover, they can not be printed on the same page with the descriptions referring to them, except at great additional expense, but must be on separate leaves.

In some respects, moreover, wood engravings, when executed in the highest style of art, are superior to those on copper or steel There is a certain indescribable boldness and richness of effect that characterizes this mode when it is carried to perfection which can not be produced on copper or steel.

In making a wood engraving, the first thing to be done is for the artist to draw the design on the block of wood to be engraved. The wood used must be of a very fine and compact grain. Boxwood is the kind generally employed. In fact, no other wood has yet been discovered with a grain close enough to serve for fine engravings. As the boxwood is a small tree, blocks of sufficient size for large engravings can be procured only by gluing together a number of pieces. It is prepared by being sawed off in blocks from the end of the log, and then squared and smoothed in a very exact manner. These operations are performed by means of very ingenious machinery, at large establishments devoted expressly to the business. The thickness of the blocks is uniform, being the same as the length of the types, in order that the blocks, when engraved, may be set up with the types in a page of matter. The size of the block, of course, varies with the size of the design.

In making the design, the artist sometimes reads the work of the author, and selects his subject, and sometimes the author himself selects the subjects, and gives the designer a description of them. The artist then makes a design and drawing corresponding to the description. To illustrate this more fully, I give here an actual description of a design, selected at random from the last set which I sent to Mr. Dopler, the artist who makes many of the drawings for these Story Books, and insert also an engraving of the design which he made, that the reader may compare them. The design belongs to a set made to illustrate a future number of the Story Books entitled JOHN TRUE. Of course this block will be used twice. It is employed here to illustrate the nature of designing. In the story, when we reach it in the series, it will come in again, in its proper place, to illustrate the narrative.

The following is the description sent:

LUNCHEON

A corner in a handsome breakfast-room in the Fifth Avenue. A small table neatly set for luncheon near a large bow window. Rich furniture partly or wholly shown. Handsome curtains to the window. Two pretty children, John True, and his sister, five years old, are at the table eating their luncheon, which consists of chicken-pie, and a tumbler of milk for each. Pitcher on the table. The children are dressed very plainly and simply.

On the facing page you will see the design which the artist made.

Specimen of a design to be compared with the description.

THE DESIGN

By comparing the description with the design, the reader will see how much in all cases is necessarily left to the inventive genius of the artist in respect to all the details of the work. Some-

Common mistake	Designing an intellectual art	Preparation of the wood

times persons imagine that being able to draw prettily upon paper or Bristol-board, from engravings or from drawings made by other persons, is evidence of qualifications to make original designs on wood for the engraver, but a very few trials will in most cases convince them how great is the mistake. The penciling is merely the mechanical part of the work. Designing, on the other hand, is purely an intellectual process, and it requires intellectual qualities of the highest order to perform it successfully. There must be a poetical fancy, great powers of invention, and a refined and delicate taste combined. The putting of the drawing on the wood is only a mechanical mode of expressing the conceptions of the mind. The success of the work will depend, of course, altogether on what the conceptions are that are expressed, and this depends on the structure of the mind, and not on the skill or training of the hand.

In other words, a designer is a *poet* whose hand has been trained to express his mental conceptions by drawing. Where the conceptions of the mind are meagre, weak, and prosaic, no skill of the hand will be of any avail, for the hand can not change the conceptions. It can only express them as they are.

In drawing on the wood, the artist first whitens the surface of the block by applying a composition to it. He usually sketches his design first in outline on paper, and then transfers the tracing to this white surface by pressure. He then goes on to finish the drawing. It would be difficult to draw on a thick block, if it were placed by itself upon a table or desk, for want of a support to the hand, especially at those parts of the design which come near the edges. To remedy this inconvenience, the artist uses a sort of drawing-board or tablet to place his block in while he is drawing upon it. This tablet consists of a board with a flat border on two sides of it. The border is about two or three inches wide, and is of the exact thickness of the block. The block is placed upon this board in the angle of the border, and thus the upper side of the border forms a continuous surface with the upper side of the block, and serves as a support to the hand in drawing.

Besides this tablet, the designer requires but few instruments or implements for his work. He must have a variety of pencils, of various degrees of hardness and blackness, and a pair of compasses, and scales of equal parts, and tracing-paper, brushes, and India ink, and a few other similar materials, and this is all. He, however, requires many aids in the way of models and patterns. It is true that, in all original designs that he makes, he must depend upon his own inventive fancy for the general conception of the scene, and for the selection and disposition of the objects that he introduces; but in drawing the details, he must have either these objects themselves before him, or else good drawings of them made by others, except in the case of those comparatively few forms which he has drawn so often that he already knows them thoroughly. This makes it necessary for him to have in his studio a great number and variety of models of forms, and also books and portfolios of engravings, and other objects and works of art, to aid him, and these generally make the studio a very attractive place.

View of Döpler's studio.

THE STUDIO.

When the artist has finished a set of designs, the blocks containing the drawings are sent to the engraver to be cut. This work of cutting consists, as has been already explained, in cutting out all the wood *between the lines* of the design, so as to leave the lines themselves in relief.

This any one not well acquainted with the subject might well suppose to be impossible, so fine are the lines, and so close together do they lie in a good drawing. Just look, for example, at the engraving of the Studio, and observe the drawing of the surface of the wall above and around the picture which hangs over the mantle-piece. The drawing consists of a series of fine lines, very near together. Now, in cutting this part of the block, the workman, with a fine and sharp-pointed tool, cuts a series of grooves, leaving the part of the wood which represents the lines in relief. You will easily imagine how nice and minute an operation this must be. And yet this is comparatively a very simple case, and very easy to be engraved. Look, for another example, at the shadows of the picture-frame on the wall, on the right-hand side of it—that is, on the side opposite the light. That shadow is made by leaving an extra line there between every two of the regular wall-shading. It will, perhaps, be necessary to examine the work with a magnifying-glass to see distinctly, though the general effect produced—that is, the appearance of a shadow, is visible at once to every eye.

It is so with every portion of the engraving. Examine it carefully in every part, and wherever you see a light part on the paper, there you may know that the wood has been cut away; and wherever you see a line or a black surface, there the wood has been left. The ink, of course, only takes effect where the wood has been left, and thus the lines and shadings of the design are printed.

Where the lines of the drawing cross each other, as they often do, there the difficulty of engraving it is greatly increased, as the wood must in those cases be cut away in the interstices of the crossings, which is an extremely nice and delicate operation.

The engraver, when engaged at his work, sits at a high table placed in a clear light. Attached to the stand on which he supports the block while he is cutting it, there is a magnifying-glass, placed in such a position as to be before his eye when he is engaged at his work. It is only quite a coarse style of engraving which can be executed with the naked eye.

The process of cutting the block is very laborious and slow. To engrave the one used for the frontispiece of this number must have required not less than ten or twelve days of incessant labor.

When the block is engraved it is sent to the compositor, and he sets it in its place in the page in which it is to be printed, having previously adjusted the thickness of it exactly to the length of the types, so that the upper surface of it may come on a level with the faces of the types, and thus the whole be printed together.

When the pages are thus made ready, the engravings being all inserted in their places, and the letter-press being made correct, they are wedged up in chases, one or more in each, according to the size of them, and are sent to the electrotyping department to be electrotyped, in the manner already explained.

CHAPTER XII.

THE PRESS.

IN the engraving on the next page we have a representation of a hand-press, of one of the most approved modern forms. The great power-presses that are driven by steam, though much larger and much more complicated in their details, are substantially the same in all their essential parts, and the principle of the machine can be more easily understood in the simpler model.

The essential parts of all printing-presses are these:

1. The Bed.
2. The Tympan.
3. The Frisket.
4. The Carriage.
5. The Platen.
6. The Power.

These will be explained in their order.

You will perceive, however, in the first instance, that the general framework of the press consists of two upright pillars supported on a stand, with a sort of table extending horizontally from the pillars toward the right. The pillars are connected together by two very solid and heavy cross-pieces, one above and one below. The upper one of these cross-pieces is called the head of the press. The lower one forms a support for the bed when the pressure is applied. The pressure being thus exerted between these two cross-pieces, of course the whole strain comes upon them, and upon the upright pillars to which they are secured. It is necessary, therefore, to have this part of the framework very strong

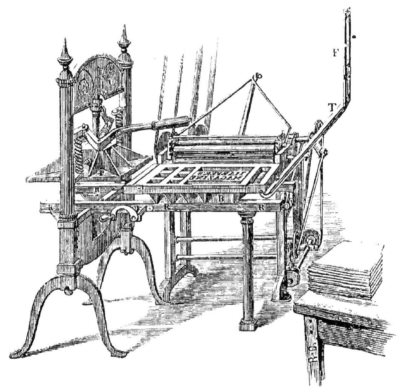

THE HAND-PRESS.

In former times, these upright pillars were made of very thick and solid beams of wood, with heavy blocks of wood, for cross-pieces, bolted and screwed firmly to them above and below. Afterward they were made of cast iron, the upright parts and the cross-pieces being all cast in one solid mass. At the present time wrought iron pillars are used, and thus the same strength is attained with a much greater degree of lightness.

The action of the press is simply as follows: B is the bed. The form to be printed is placed upon it. In the engraving, the press is represented as prepared for printing one of the large placards for Harper's Magazine. We see the words in the form as it lies in its place upon the bed. The words are, of course, reversed, but they will come right when printed, or when seen in a looking-glass. T is the tympan. The sheet to be printed is placed upon it. F is the frisket. The use of the frisket is to hold the sheet close upon the tympan when the tympan is turned over upon the form. The frisket is a light iron frame, covered with paper, and moving on hinges, with openings in the paper to correspond with the pages of the form that is to be printed. When the sheet is placed upon the tympan, the frisket is brought down over it, to hold the paper, and then the tympan is brought down to the form. Of course, the paper comes over the face of the types, which have been previously inked by the rollers seen behind, and the tympan comes upon the back of it. The tympan consists of a piece of India-rubber cloth stretched upon a frame, with one thickness of flannel or something similar placed behind it, and kept in its place by a lining of muslin. Its object is to equalize, as it were, the pressure upon the sheet of paper on the form.

And now the bed of the press, B, carrying the form, with the tympan and frisket folded over it, is run backward along the rails, R, R, on a sort of concealed carriage, worked by a crank, seen in the side of the rail, until it is under the platen, P. This platen is simply a thick iron plate, strongly braced, and arranged so as to be movable through a short space up and down. L is a lever connected with a joint which furnishes the power for pressing the platen down. It is worked by means of the long handle extending to the right. The pressman runs the form in under the platen with his left hand by means of the crank, and then, with his right hand, pulls the handle, and forces the platen down with very great power upon the tympan, thus pressing the sheet hard upon the face of the types, and causing it to take the impression. Then pushing back the handle, the two spiral springs seen above on each side lift the platen up, and the form is released. The pressman

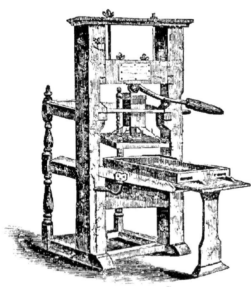

FRANKLIN'S PRESS.

then runs the form out, as he had run it in, by turning the little side crank, and, unfolding the frisket and tympan, he takes out the sheet and puts in another. While he is doing this, the roller, seen behind, by means of some curious machinery connected with it, comes forward, and inks the form so as to be ready for a new impression.

The adjoining engraving is a correct representation of one of the presses used by Franklin before the Revolution. It is of comparatively very rude construction, but the reader will observe that the same essential parts are to be seen in it that have been described. The frisket is folded down, and so does not appear; but the tympan is there, and the bed, and the carriage, and the platen, and the power, which in this case is a screw.

The great difference in the mechanism of the two machines illustrates in some measure the immense progress that has been made in the course of the last half century in the mechanical arts; and yet, to get a full and complete idea of this progress, we must compare Franklin's press, not with the hand-press already described, but with one of the great power-presses, by means of which almost all the prodigious printing operations of the present day are performed. A representation of one of these presses, as it stands in the great press-room of the Harper Establishment, is seen in the following page. It is too complicated to be fully described in detail, but some of the more prominent features of it may be pointed out. The girl who stands at it is called the feeder. She has a pile of damped paper on a stand over the press. The pile is inclined a little toward her, so as to make it easier for her to draw off the successive sheets. Under this pile of paper is the platen. We recognize it by the iron braces partially seen beneath the stand on which the paper is placed. The form is beneath the platen, and is not in view. It rests there on the bed of the press, which is likewise hidden. To the right, we see a part of the system of rollers by which the form is inked. The feeder has just placed a sheet to be printed on the inclined table before her. This

THE POWER-PRESS.

table is called the *apron*. In a moment a set of iron fingers will come up from below, and, taking hold of the lower edge of the paper, will draw it in under the platen, between the platen and the form. The revolution of the machinery will then bring an immense power into operation, by means of cams and levers seen below, by which the bed of the press, with the form and sheet upon it, are pressed up for a moment with great force against the platen. This makes the impression. The form then descends again, and the sheet, by a very ingenious and peculiar mechanism, passes out *under* the apron on which the feeder originally placed it, toward the left, where the edge of it jumps up very mysteriously upon a series of endless tapes, which may be seen in the engraving through the fly-wheel.* From these it is taken up by a light frame, formed of long and slender rods of wood, and is carried over and laid down upon the pile at the extreme left of the engraving. Thus the work goes regularly on, with no attendance whatever except the placing of each successive sheet within the reach of the iron fingers which are to draw it into the machine.

Visitors who watch the motions of the press while it is performing its work are always particularly pleased with the life-like actions of the iron fingers that come up and take hold of the lower edge of the sheet of paper on the apron, and, after lifting it gently over the *ledge* formed on the lower side of the apron to prevent its

---

* The term *endless*, when used in such a connection as this, in the description of machinery, denotes that the band, or chain, or whatever else it may be to which it is applied, passes over two pulleys at a distance from each other, and is joined at the ends, so as to revolve continuously between and over the pulleys

sliding down, draw it in under the platen to be printed; and
when the sheet comes out again, under the apron, after receiving
the impression, they wonder by what means the edge of it is made
to leap up so dexterously upon the tape-lines that are to carry it
away.   They often watch this motion very closely a long while
without being able to discover how the effect is produced.   The
explanation is, that the edge of the sheet is *blown* up by a puff of
wind from below.   There is a pair of bellows concealed in the
frame-work of the press, and at precisely the right instant the revolution of the machinery gives a puff from it up through a row of
holes exactly under the edge of the sheet of paper.   The impulse
of this puff throws the edge of the sheet up to the tapes, and the
long fingers of the frame which is to lift it over and place it upon
the pile having previously laid themselves between the tapes, the
sheet is received upon them, and immediately afterward is carried
over.   In the engraving, this frame, which is called a fly, has just
carried over one printed sheet, and is coming back for another.

There are nearly thirty of these presses in the great press-room,
and there is something imposing and almost sublime in the calm
and steady dignity with which the ponderous engines continue
their ceaseless toil.   There is, indeed, a real dignity and a real
grace in the movements which they perform.   The observer looks
down the room from the elevated desk of the foreman, and surveys
the scene with great interest and pleasure, wondering at the complicated massiveness of the constructions, and at the multitude of
wheels, and pulleys, and bands that mingle and combine their motions with the revolutions of the machinery.   His attention is

particularly attracted to the action of the *flus*, as they rise in succession, one after another, in all parts of the room, bringing up the beautifully printed sheets from the press, and, carrying them over, lay them gently down upon the gradually accumulating pile.

When all the forms of the book which is in hand have been "worked off," as the phrase is, the electrotype plates of the several pages, having been previously separated from the blocks, are taken back to the subterranean vaults, and are there safely stored away in the compartments assigned to them. The place of the entrance to these vaults was shown, and some account of their extent was given, in a previous chapter. The number of plates accumulated there, enormous as it is, is increasing at the rate of, upon an average, two hundred a day.

CHAPTER XIII.

DRYING AND PRESSING THE SHEETS.

SHEETS of paper to be printed require, as has already been remarked, to be made damp before being put upon the press. When perfectly dry, they do not take the ink well. Of course, after they are printed, the first process is to dry them.

Newspapers are not dried, but are distributed to the subscribers just as they come from the press. There is not time to dry them, for they must ordinarily be issued immediately. But sheets which are to be folded and formed into books require to be dried and then to be pressed. This pressing is necessary, not only for the purpose of flattening out the warpings and twistings in the sheets, produced by their having been wet and dried, but also to remove the little burr or protrusion in the paper made by the pressure of the types.

The process of drying the sheets has already been referred to, and the place where it is performed is shown in the section on page 42. It is in the second story, and in the first division of that story toward the left. The opposite engraving gives an enlarged view of the drying apparatus. The men on the left are bringing the sheets to be dried. They take them down from a stack of sheets piled up in the racks so high that it requires a ladder to reach them. The sheets are moved from place to place about the floor by means of trucks. One of these trucks stands by itself in the foreground. In the centre of the picture, three men are employed in placing the sheets upon one of the frames, which has been drawn out for the purpose from the drying-room. The workmen put the sheets on the lowermost bars of the frame with their hands. The higher bars are reached by means of a pole, with a cross-bar at the top of it. The form of this instrument, and the manner in which the workmen load it with the sheets—several at a time—is seen by the action of the man who is standing at the truck, near the frame. When the sheets are put upon the pole in this way, they are lifted up and placed across the upper bars of the frame, as we see in the action of the central figure of the group.

When all the bars of the frames are filled with sheets, the frame itself is pushed into the drying compartment. The end of each frame consists of a board of the same width as the distance at which the frames stand apart when they are in their places, and

Construction and arrangement of the drying-room

THE DRYING-ROOM.

thus these boards, when the frames are all in, form one continuous partition, which shuts off the compartment closely from the rest of the room, and keeps the hot air within it confined till the sheets are dried. Of course, there is a proper arrangement for ventilation, in order that the vapors produced by the process of drying may be carried away.

View of the hydraulic presses.

Account of the hydraulic pump and of the hydraulic presses

There are over forty of these frames in the compartment. They will contain twelve hundred sheets each, making about fifty thousand sheets in all that may be dried at one time. The process of drying requires about a day.

The frames can be moved in and out very easily, for they are all suspended by pulleys or trucks, that run upon little railways placed near the ceiling above.

When the sheets are dried they are to be pressed. The pressure is applied by means of a hydraulic pump. A view of this engine is seen on the right, in the foreground. Though it does not appear large in the engraving, the force of pressure which it exerts is not less than five hundred tons. It consists simply of a double-acting force-pump, with cylinders of small bore, but with a great force from the engine to act upon the pistons. This forces the water through a very strong pipe beneath the floor to other cylinders, fitted also with pistons, under the presses. These other cylinders are large. Of course, whatever force is applied to the small pistons in the pumps, an equal amount of pressure is produced on every square inch of the large pistons in the cylinders under the presses, and thus a prodigious pressure on the sheets of paper is the result.

We see the upper part of one of these large cylinders under the first of the presses on the left. Above it is a square iron plate, which forms a base on which the pile of sheets of paper to be pressed rests. This plate, like those of similar function in the printing-press, is called the platen. It is very thick, and is stiffened beneath by iron braces, which are partially seen in the en-

graving.   The little circular handle which is seen rising up out of
the floor, opposite the end of the press, is connected with a valve,
by which the water in the great cylinders may be let off, and the
pressure relieved.

The presses themselves stand in a row at the end of the room.
They occupy the right hand of the second story of the building,
as shown in a sectional view of the different stories on page 42.
Each press may be connected with the pump, or disconnected from
it at pleasure, so that one may be giving up or receiving a supply
of sheets while the others are full and in action.

The manner of placing the sheets in the press is shown in the
engraving, where a man is seen at the third press in the row, standing on a step-ladder, and making up the pile.   The arrangement
for taking this pile out when it has been sufficiently pressed is exceedingly ingenious and convenient.   In front of the row of presses
is a little railway, as seen in the engraving.   This railway is trav-
ersed by two small cars, one of which is seen distinctly in the
foreground.   The other is in the distance, and is partly concealed.
These cars serve the purpose of bridges to convey the piles of
pressed paper *across* the railway, or as cars to move *along* it, as
may be required.   For this purpose, two short rails are laid across
each of them.   We see these cross-rails very distinctly in the
bridge which stands in the foreground.   By means of these cross-
rails, the whole pile of paper may be run out upon the bridge ; for
the pile itself, while in the press, rests upon trucks and rails above
the platen, which are, however, concealed from view.   The machinery is so arranged that when the bridge is placed opposite one

The railways	The flying bridges	Pasteboard sheets

of the presses, the rails on the bridge correspond exactly with the rails on the platen in the press, which the pile of paper rests upon, and also with the rails of a square stand placed opposite, just outside the long rails. We see one of these stands, with a low pile of paper upon it, where the boy is at work taking the paper away.

In a word, by trundling the bridge along the railway in the floor, it may be placed in such a manner as to form a railway above, running *across* from the presses to the stand outside, by means of which the whole pile of pressed sheets may be rolled out at once to a situation where the boys can come conveniently to take them away, while, in the mean time, the press itself is at liberty to be filled up at once again.

These facilities for moving the masses of paper are the more necessary, on account of the great quantity that the presses receive at a time. The stack is nearly six feet high, and weighs about a ton.

Each sheet, when it is put into the press, is placed between two sheets of thin, but very smooth and hard pasteboard. It is very plain that the sheets would not be pressed smooth by coming in juxtaposition with each other. The processes of putting the sheets in between these pasteboards, and taking them out again after they are pressed, is quite an interesting one, on account of the very systematic and rapid manner in which it is performed. Opposite the presses, and just beyond the right-hand margin of the last engraving, there stands a range of very wide tables where this work is done. It requires two men at each table to do it. One takes out from between two sheets of pasteboard the sheet of paper that has been pressed, and the other, at the same instant almost, puts another in, shifting the several sheets, both of paper and pasteboard, from pile to pile, in the course of the manipulation, with a dexterity and rapidity that is surprising. As fast as a sufficient number of the rearranged sheets are ready, a boy takes them away, and places them in the press, while another boy continually brings a fresh supply of those that have been pressed to take their places.

The pressing which the sheets receive in this operation makes an astonishing difference in the smoothness and beauty of the page when the book comes to be bound.

CHAPTER XIV.

FORWARDING.

WHEN the sheets are folded, they are *gathered*, as it is termed; that is, a pile of each sort being laid out along a table, a girl takes from each pile one, and puts them together in the proper order, so as to form the book or pamphlet.

These separate sheets are all marked at the foot of the outer page of each of them with what is called the *signature*, that is, with a letter or figure which denotes what sheet it is of the series. The girl glances her eye at these signatures when gathering the sheets, and thus makes sure that there is no mistake, but that she is taking them in their proper order. You will see these signatures in this book by looking at the foot of the pages following every sixteenth page—that is, at the foot of pages 17, 33, 49, &c. You will observe that the letters succeed each other in regular order.

If the work is a pamphlet, as, for example, a number of the Magazine or of the Story Books, it is *stitched*. If it is a bound book, it is to be *sewed*.

STABBING.

To prepare the pamphlet for stitching, three holes are made through the sheets by means of a machine called a *stabbing machine*. The pamphlet to be stabbed is laid by the workman upon a flat board, and then, by means of a pedal, or lever, worked by the foot, three steel points are brought down through the paper, so as to make the three holes required for the twine by which the pamphlet is to be stitched. You will see these holes, and the twine passing through them, by examining any pamphlet.

Books that are to be bound are *sewed*, as it is called: this is quite a different process from stitching. To prepare the books for being sewed, the first step is to *saw* small grooves through the backs of them, deep enough to receive the bands of twine to which each sheet is secured. The sawing of these grooves is performed in what is called a sawing machine. This machine consists of a table, with two iron rails upon it running from end to end. On these rails is a sort of box, or rather frame, with sides and back,

View of the machine for sawing the backs.

THE SAWING MACHINE.

but no front. This frame traverses the table to and fro on the rails. The workman takes a quantity of folded sheets from a supply made ready for him on the tables near, and, placing them in this frame, he wedges them in securely. Beneath the table are placed several circular saws, arranged at the proper distance from each other. The teeth of these saws project a little above the table, through an opening made in it, in such a manner that, when the frame is run along over them, the grooves are sawed in the backs of the sheets.

The sheets are then to be sewed. This operation is performed by great numbers of girls, seated at long tables, extending in rows along the room, as shown in the sectional view in page 42. The sewing of the books is a great work. The ranges of tables devoted to it are so extensive as to furnish accommodations for one hundred girls, and each place is provided with a seat and a stool, that may both be raised or depressed, to suit the comfort and convenience of the occupant.* Every visitor who sees these girls at their work is struck with the extreme rapidity and dexterity of their movements, and with the healthy, and happy, and highly attractive appearance which they themselves and the scene of their labors exhibit. Indeed, so far as my observation goes, one of the chief subjects of remark with strangers, after coming away from a visit to the whole establishment, is the intelligent and manly bearing of the men who are employed in it, and the attractive appearance and lady-like manners of the girls.

* The number of girls employed in the gilding-room is 12, in the sewing room 100; in the gathering and folding-room, 150; and in the press-room 30, making nearly 300 in all.

View of the cutting machine and of the great shears.

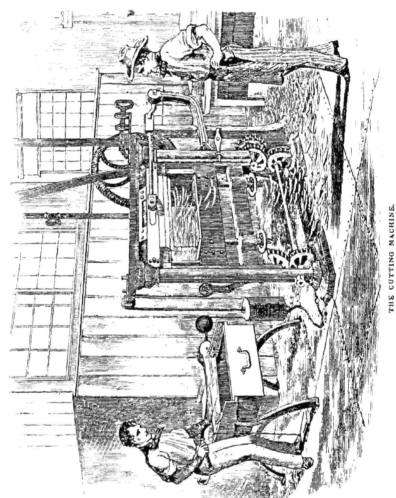

THE CUTTING MACHINE.

On the opposite page is an engraving of one of the different kinds of machines by which the edges of the books, when sewed, are trimmed. A pile of the books is screwed up very tight in a massive frame, as seen in the engraving, and then a long and straight blade of steel is made to traverse to and fro with great rapidity, the frame gradually rising, as the blade cuts its way through the pile of books, until the edges of the whole pile are trimmed smooth. The books are then turned, and the same operation is repeated on the ends.

The great shears seen in operation at one side are used for cutting up sheets of pasteboard to form covers for the books.

These preliminary processes, which all belong to the department of binding called *forwarding*, are performed chiefly in the fifth story of the Cliff Street building, as is shown more plainly in the sectional view.

CHAPTER XV.

MARBLING.

In a corner of the forwarding apartment there is a small inclosure, partially separated from the rest of the room by low partitions, that is appropriated to the process of *marbling*. This is one of the most curious processes to be seen in the whole establishment. There are two forms of it—one the marbling of sheets of paper, and the other that of the edges of books. The process is essentially the same in both cases. It consists of sprinkling the colors first upon the surface of a liquid, in a sort of tank, and then taking them off upon the surface to be marbled by bringing the paper, or the edges of the book, down gently upon the colors, and thus, as it were, *sponging* them up from off the surface of the liquid on which they were floating.

One would suppose that such an operation as this would be perfectly impossible, and visitors who witness it for the first time regard it with astonishment and delight.

THE MARBLING-ROOM.

The engraving represents a workman in the act of taking up a sheet of paper which he had just before laid down upon the surface of the liquid in the tank. On the right is a bench containing the pots of colors. They are mixed with water, and are of the proper consistency to sprinkle easily from a brush. They contain, however, some composition which prevents their blending with each other when sprinkled, one after another, upon the surface of the liquid in the tank. Each drop, when falling upon the spot made by the preceding drop, instead of mixing with it, remains perfectly distinct, only crowding the color of the preceding drop away a little to make room for itself, as we shall presently see.

The pots contain but a small quantity of coloring matter, little more than enough to cover the bottom of them. If it were otherwise, too much would be taken up by the brushes. The brushes themselves are of somewhat peculiar form, the bristles extending laterally more than is usual. When the surface of the liquid in the tank is ready to receive the sprinkling, the workman takes one of the brushes, and rolls it between his hands, by the handle, before he takes it out of the pot, in order to throw off the superfluous coloring from it; and then, holding it over the tank, he proceeds to sprinkle the surface of the liquid with it, throwing off minute drops from the brush by a peculiar and very dexterous motion. The drops fall upon the surface of the liquid in the tank like drops of rain upon a pond, only, instead of sinking and disappearing, they remain on the surface, spreading into pretty large and exceedingly well defined and beautiful circular spots of red, blue, green, or violet, as the case may be. The drops spread, some of them to the size of a quarter of a dollar, and are almost mathematically perfect in their form.

The workman then takes another brush from another pot, and

SPRINKLING THE COLORS.

sprinkles the surface again with another color.   If the first color was red, the second may perhaps be blue.   In this case, the blue drops, instead of mingling with the red, remain perfectly distinct from them, crowding them, moreover, more or less out of their places, and modifying the forms of them.   For example, if a blue drop were to fall directly upon the centre of a red spot that was produced by the previous sprinkling, it would crowd out the red color to a wider circumference, while it would itself occupy the

centre, and we should have, in that case, a central blue spot surrounded by a concentric ring of red. On the other hand, if the
blue drop were to fall upon the margin of the red drop, then it
would push one half of the red spot back upon itself, straightening
the side that it came in contact with, and expanding the opposite
side. The result would be, in this case, a large circular spot, one
half of which would be blue and the other half red, the boundary
between the two being a straight line passing from one side of the
spot, through the centre, to the other side. Of course, it is not
often that either of these two cases precisely occurs. The drops
of blue fall indiscriminately all over the surface of the liquid in the
tank, and come upon the drops of red in every variety of position,
producing, consequently, an infinite variety of forms by the combinations of the two colors.

In the mean time, the workman continues the process of sprinkling. He takes next some other color : it may be yellow, or green,
or dark purple. Whatever it may be, the third set of drops fall
as the others did, each making for itself a place by crowding the
others out of the way, and producing new and still more complicated varieties of form. This sprinkling is followed by another
and another, until at length there may be five, six, or eight different colors combined, and then, on closely examining the surface,
you will perceive that the original red is still entirely distinct from
the colors that have been subsequently added, not having *mingled*
with them at all, even at the lines of contact with them, though
the form of the spaces which it occupies is entirely changed. The
original circles have entirely disappeared, and the red is now seen

occupying only the curved and irregular interstices which lie between the drops formed by subsequent sprinklings.   In a word,
the whole surface of the liquid in the tank has become covered
with brilliant and variegated colors, each different, one being separated from the next by distinct and well-defined lines, that wave
and curve among each other in beautiful and endlessly-varied configurations.

The reader will understand all this much better by examining
some piece of marble paper, if he can find a specimen at hand.
By counting the number of colors, you can ascertain how many
sprinklings were required for that particular sheet, and by observ-
ing the forms of the different masses of color in the light of the
explanation given above, you can almost determine the precise order in which the different sprinklings were applied.

Sometimes the arrangement of the colors on the liquid in the
tank is modified in a very curious way by drawing a sort of rake
or comb along the surface of it.   The instruments used for this
purpose are of different kinds, varying in the fineness of the teeth,
and in their distance from each other.   These teeth, being drawn
over the surface of the liquid in the tank, have the effect of *drawing* the colors, as they term it, and thus modifying the configurations in a very curious manner, producing a sort of honey-combed
or scalloped appearance very difficult to describe, but which those
who have seen it will easily remember.   This is called the comb
pattern.

When at length the sprinkled surface is ready, the workman
takes a sheet of white paper, supposing that it is marbled *paper*

that he now wishes to produce, and lays it carefully down upon
the liquid, beginning at one corner, and letting the sheet gradually
down until it lies wholly on the liquid. He then immediately
proceeds to apply a second sheet, the tank being of a size to receive two sheets at a time. He then takes the two sheets up
again, one after the other, when it is found that the beautifully
variegated colors which have been floating on the liquid have been
wholly transferred to the sheets. They have been taken up by
the paper, and so completely absorbed, too, into the substance of
it, that the surface, all wet and dripping as it is, may be rubbed
with the finger without in any degree disturbing the colors. The
sheets, as they are taken up, are laid across a wooden rod, and
hung upon a frame near by to drain and dry. We see the frame
in the engraving, with the sheets hanging on it, to the left of the
workman.

Of course, the number of patterns which can be formed by the
different combinations of colors, and the different modes of applying them, are infinitely varied. If, for example, all the colors that
are to be used in the pattern are applied to the liquid before the
comb is drawn over the surface of it, then one effect will be produced; but if one of the colors is reserved until after the combing,
and then sprinkled on, the effect, as may easily be seen, would be
totally different, and this difference may be varied by reserving
any one of the dozen different colors that are to be applied. And
so with every other step in the complicated process.

There is one peculiar pattern, called the *wave* pattern. It is
characterized by a series of waves in the coloring. The waves

succeed each other at short and regular intervals, passing diagonally across the sheet. This effect is produced simply by the mode of laying the sheet upon the colors. The workman begins at one corner; but then, instead of letting the successive portions of the paper down by a slow and uniform motion, he gives it, very dexterously, a series of gentle impulses, letting down the paper a short space at each impulse. This occasions a sort of fluctuation on the surface of the liquid, and the colors, whatever they may be, are taken up in waves.

Then, besides the fine combs, there are large and coarse ones, with teeth several inches apart, by means of which the colors may be *drawn* in various ways over the surface of the liquid, so as to produce the appearance of streams, and an endless variety of other beautiful configurations.

It will easily be seen that the number of patterns which may be formed by the different combinations of these and other similar elements is literally infinite, and, of course, to be a good marbler, a man must possess excellent judgment and taste, as well as great skill.

The beautiful gloss which we see upon finished marble paper does not appear upon it when it first comes from the marbler's hands. This gloss is the result of a subsequent process of *burnishing*, which is represented by the engraving on the opposite page.

The burnishing is produced by means of a piece of polished flint or agate, which passes rapidly to and fro over the surface of

View of the burnishing machine in action.

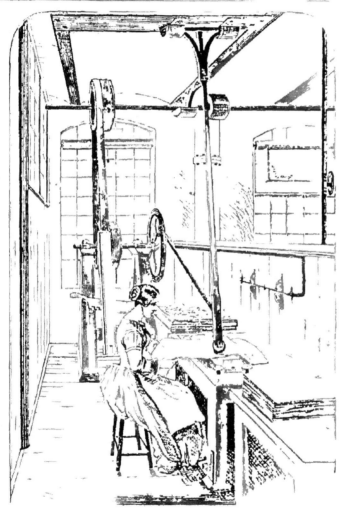

BURNISHING.

the paper, the sheet being held for the purpose upon a sort of bed prepared for it to lie upon, on a very solid bench or table.   The burnisher, as is shown in the engraving, is attached to the lower end of a long lever that descends from the ceiling.   At the upper end of the lever is a joint, by means of which the lower end may be moved to and fro.   Near the lower end is a bar, which may be seen passing off toward the window, where it is attached to a crank on the outer side of the wheel.   When the axle of that wheel is put in motion by means of the band coming down from above and passing over the pulleys—seen at the left-hand end of the axle— the crank is turned, and the bar pulls the burnisher to and fro very rapidly over the surface of the paper.

The bed on which the paper rests while undergoing the opera- tion is a block of wood set in a frame that is screwed to the bench. The end of it is seen in the engraving under the sheet of paper. The upper surface of this block is made concave, so that the bur- nisher, in moving to and fro, shall always be in contact with it. This bed is not absolutely fixed, but is susceptible of being moved up and down, so as to press with a greater or less degree of force against the burnisher, as may be required.   This pressure is reg- ulated by means of a strong spring connected with a pedal below.

As the process of burnishing goes on, the operator draws the sheet forward by a very slow and careful motion, so as to subject all parts of it in succession to the polishing effect of the friction. It requires considerable skill to manage the sheet so as to produce upon it a smooth and uniform gloss.   The operator, in holding the sheet, begins in the middle of it, and works first toward the farther side by drawing the sheet gently forward as the process goes on. She then turns the sheet, and, taking the half already polished toward her, she proceeds with the operation on the other half in the same manner.

Not only marble paper, but colored papers of all kinds are burnished in this manner.

CHAPTER XVI.

FINISHING.

WHEN books are to be bound in muslin, the covers of them are not formed upon the book itself, but are made and finished separately, and are afterward applied to the book and properly secured. These covers, before they are applied to the book, are called *cases*. They are made in great quantities by a series of separate processes, each workman performing one process upon a great number of covers, and then passing the whole stock into the hands of another workman for the next process.

Thus one cuts out the pasteboard for the sides of the cover by means of the great shears shown in a previous engraving. The frame to which the shears are fixed is so made that the pasteboard is measured by the very operation of cutting it. The workman has only to slide the sheet along as far as it will go, and then cut. He is sure to cut it in the right place without any thought or care. By this plan, the work is not only performed more rapidly and easily, but also far more exactly, than would be possible by any other method of measuring. The sides thus cut, too, are precisely

13 K

of the same size, and they are afterward trimmed so square and true that, when they are piled up upon each other on the table, they seem to form, as it were, one solid block, like a block of wood standing on end.

Another workman cuts out the muslin or the leather, whichever it may be, that the book is to be covered with. This operation is performed with so much system, and with such excellent arrangements for facilitating it, that the work is done with astonishing rapidity and precision.

Then the parts of the case are put together. The back, connecting the two sides, is formed, and the sides are covered upon the outside, and lined within. The case is now finished as to its form, and it is taken into the stamping-room to be lettered, and also embossed or gilded on the sides or back.

In the engraving on the opposite page, a pile of covers or cases, such as are used for the bound volumes of Harper's Magazine, or any other volume of that size, are seen lying on the table in the foreground on the left. Other piles of a smaller size are seen upon the tables, where the girls are at work upon them. The employment of these girls is to apply the gold leaf to the covers in the process of gilding them with the lettering and the ornaments of various kinds with which the backs of handsomely-bound books are usually embellished.

The manner in which these gilded letters and ornaments are made is very curious. To illustrate and explain it, I will take a very simple case. Let us suppose that a book is to have its title —one single word, we will say—put on in gilded letters on the

GILDING.

back, and that this word is to be put in letters of such a size that it will occupy a space about half an inch wide directly across the back of the book, at a proper distance from the top. The cover is brought to the table seen in the engraving. One of the girls, with a small piece of sponge, which she has dipped previously in a certain preparation, formed chiefly of the white of an egg, of which she has a supply before her ready for use, moistens that part of the cover where the lettering is to come. She then cuts out a strip of gold leaf half an inch wide, and long enough to extend across the back of the book, and places it upon the part which she has moistened. It adheres a little, and forms a gilded stripe across the case in the place where the letters should appear.

This is what the girls are doing at the long table in the preceding engraving. They are putting on strips of gold on all those parts of the cases of the books where the letters or the ornaments are to come. They keep their supplies of gold leaf in the drawers. They have an apparatus, of the form of a little stool, on the table before them, to work upon, and they use a variety of curious implements for dividing and moving the gold leaf, which is so thin and light that the least breath of wind would blow it away. Indeed, so great is the danger of this, that they are obliged to have a sort of screen placed before them on the table, to shelter their work from the accidental draughts which might be produced in the room by an open window, or by persons walking to and fro. This screen consists of some transparent texture spread over a frame. Thus it does not intercept the light, while yet it protects the work from the slightest movement of the air.

But let us return to the cover, which was to be gilded with its title only on the back. When it has had placed upon it the strip of leaf large enough for the title, it is taken to a kind of press to be stamped. In this press is what is called a *die*—that is, a block of metal with the letters of the title of the book cut upon it in relief, precisely as the letters are cut upon the ends of the steel

The die	Effect of it.	Manner of fixing the gold

punches used in type-founding, as has already been described
This die is made hot when it is placed in the press by means of
steam circulating in concealed channels around it.   The case is
then slipped in, and it is placed with the face downward under it,
and that instant the bed of the press rises by the action of the
machinery, and forces the case against the die.   Every thing is so
adjusted beforehand that, in coming up, the faces of the letters are
brought to bear with great force upon the strip of gold leaf which
had previously been laid upon the case.   There are two distinct
effects produced by the operation. First, the substance of the
leather or the muslin that comes directly upon the face of the letters in the die is compressed, and an *indentation* is made—one
not very deep, it is true, but still very certain and distinct.   And,
secondly, the heat of the die causes the gold leaf to adhere where
it touches—that is, where the faces of the letters come, while it has
no effect on the other parts.   Thus that portion of the gold leaf
which corresponds with the letters is forced, as it were, into in-
dentations in the muslin or the leather, and fixed there by the heat
and pressure of the die, while all the rest of it remains at liberty,
and may be wiped away by a cloth, or a cushioned brush of soft
leather.   The cover, when it is first withdrawn from the press,
looks very much as it did when it went in, the forms of the letters
being at first scarcely visible; but, on wiping away the superfluous gold leaf, they come out fully to view, distinctly defined, and
extremely brilliant and beautiful.

One would at first suppose that this must be a very wasteful
mode of making gilded letters, inasmuch as so large a portion of

the leaf first applied has afterward to be brushed or wiped away.
It is true that only a small part of the whole strip which the girl
first puts on the cover remains imprinted there by the action of the
die, for the space lying between the letters, and above and below
them, is much greater than that occupied by the faces of the letters themselves.   But then the portion of the leaf that is removed
is by no means wasted or lost.   The wiping away of the superfluous gold is performed at a table well protected from currents of
air, and having holes in it that communicate with a drawer below.
The gold leaf that is rubbed off from the covers of the books passes down through these holes into the drawer, and once in three
months it is sent to the goldsmith and sold for old gold.   So great
is the amount of gilding done at this table, that the value of the
rubbish, as it might be called, which accumulates here every three
months is not less than three hundred dollars, making twelve
hundred dollars a year.

The engraving on the opposite page shows the form of the
press used for the stamping process just described.   It is made
very solid and massive, as the force of the pressure which is often
required is enormously great.   There is a massive top, which is
called the platen, the function of it being the same as that of a
platen of a printing-press, namely, to stand against the pressure
of the bed rising from below.   This top is supported, or rather *held
down*, by four wrought iron pillars, two of which are seen in the
engraving. It is obvious that the chief purpose of these pillars
is to hold the platen down rather than to hold it up, for when the
bed below rises at the time of stamping or embossing a case, it

View of one of the presses used for stamping and embossing.

EMBOSSING PRESSES.

lifts, so to speak, with prodigious force against the platen, and if the columns that hold it were not very strong, and the bolts and screws by which it is fastened to them were not very secure, it would be forced upward bodily and broken away.

The die which contains the letters or ornaments that are to be stamped upon the case is placed in the platen. It is inserted in a receptacle used for it in the under side of the platen, and properly secured there. There is a circulation of steam in channels within the platen, as has already been intimated, which serves to keep the die always hot.

Cases can be stamped in these processes at the rate of sixteen impressions a minute—that is, as fast as a man can put the cases in and take them away; and that without regard to the amount of gilding that may be required, whether it be only a single line, or whether the case be completely covered.

Sometimes the covers of books are embossed with ornamental figures impressed into the leather or muslin without gilding. The patterns for this embossing are cut in solid brass plates of the size of the cover to which they are to be applied. A great number of these plates are seen in the engraving, on the shelves at the end of the room.

When the die for gilding, or the side plate, as the case may be, is fixed in its proper position in the platen, the workman, with a pile of cases at hand, sets the machine in motion, and the bed—that is, the solid mass of iron which forms the central part of the block which the man's hands are resting upon, is forced upward by means of what is called a *knee-joint* below. The position of this knee-joint may be seen in the engraving, underneath the bed of the press. This sort of joint is often used in presses. It is sometimes called a *toggle* joint. The operation of it may be illustrated in this way. Suppose a man to stand with his back against a wall, and then to bend his knees a little forward. Of course, by bending his knees, his head is made to descend. Imagine now that a by-stander pushed his knees in, back to their place, so as to straighten his legs. His head will be forced up again. It would be forced up, too, with great power—that is, provided the man be made of iron, and with no joints in him except those at his knees, and if they are bent only a little. It is true, his head would be forced up only a very short distance, but though that short distance it would rise with great force.

This is exactly the operation of a knee or toggle joint. Look in the lower part of the press in the engraving, and you will see the iron knees. They are bent a little, for the bed of the press is now down. A man is just putting a case in. In a moment the knees will be straightened by means of a wheel connected with a steam-engine acting on a case. The consequence will be, that the bed will be forced upward. It is curious, too, that as the knees become more and more nearly straightened, the force with which the bed rises becomes more and more powerful, until at the last instant, when the knees are just arriving at absolute straightness, it becomes enormous. This ultimate force may, moreover, be regulated at pleasure by bringing the platen down or raising it up a little. The platen, and consequently the die or side-plate which it contains, may be adjusted in this way by means of an apparatus above.   There is a horizontal wheel to be seen at the top of the press, which is connected with a system of wheels and screws so contrived that the workman, by stepping up upon some support, and turning this wheel one way or the other, may raise or depress the platen so as to regulate the pressure that comes upon it at his will.   The screws hold it firmly wherever he sees fit to place it.

There are two gauges on the bed of the press, one at the side and one at the end, which regulate the position of the case when it is put into the press, and cause it to take the impression in precisely the right manner.

When books are to be bound in leather, they are finished in a different way.   In this case, the bands to which the sheets are sewed are fastened securely to the sides of the cases, and the cases are then covered, lined, and finished while attached to the book. The engraving on the opposite page gives a view of the room where these operations are performed.   It is called the finishing-room. The gilding upon the books is applied by hand, though the general principle of the process is the same as in the case of those stamped in the machine.   The furnaces seen upon the tables are used for heating the stamps by which the gilding is fixed.   The fire in these furnaces is a flame of gas diffused over a considerable surface on the bottom of the furnace within.   The manner of using the stamps in gilding the backs of the books is seen by the position of the figure in the foreground, at the end of the central table.

VIEW OF THE INTERIOR OF THE FINISHING-ROOM.

CHAPTER XVII.

THE DISTRIBUTION.

IN order to have always on hand a sufficient supply of copies of the many hundreds of works published by the house, so as to be able promptly to fill the orders from the trade as they come in, very extensive store-rooms are required to contain the books. In the early part of this volume, an explanation was given of the situation and arrangement of the bins—in number almost a thousand—in which the supplies of finished books are kept; that is, those bound, complete, ready for delivery. But these are not by any means the most considerable portion of the stores kept on hand. The principal part of the edition of any book that is printed is kept in a partially finished state in respect to binding, and is then completed in quantities as copies may be required.

The view on the following page represents one of the ware-rooms where this unfinished stock is stored. It is situated on one of the upper floors of the Franklin Square building, across the court from the sewing-room, which is on a floor nearly corresponding to it in the Cliff Street building. The sheets of each new edition of any work, after being dried, pressed, folded, gathered, and stitched or sewed, so as to be ready to be finished at very short notice, are trundled over one of the iron bridges that leads across the court, and are deposited in this ware-room. They are placed —the sheets of each work by themselves—in bins, similar to those

The stock-room.   View of one of the principal avenues in it.

THE STOCK-ROOM.

used in the ware-rooms for finished work below. These bins are built up from the floor to the ceiling, and stand in ranges, divided by passages that cross each other at right angles, and furnish very convenient access to every portion of the stores. It is only a very small part of the room that is shown in the engraving. There are two principal avenues, one hundred and thirty feet long, passing through it from end to end, only one of which is here seen.

As fast as is necessary, the unfinished books are taken from these bins, in quantities of hundreds or thousands, as the case may be, and conveyed across the bridge again to the bindery to be finished. Then they are sent down by the hoistway to the great sales-room below, to replenish the bins assigned to them there which have been emptied, or nearly emptied, by previous sales.

In this lower store-room is performed the work of selecting and packing the books ordered by the correspondents of the house, and sending them away. Every morning a large pile of letters comes in from the mail from booksellers, committee-men, librarians, directors of public institutions, teachers, and gentlemen in private life, containing lists of the books which they wish the house to forward to them. These lists are handed to the clerks, who proceed to collect the books required for each, and to arrange and pack them.

One of the principal operations of this department is the monthly distribution of the edition of the Magazine, which consists, at the present time, in round numbers, of one hundred and forty thousand copies. Few persons have any idea how large a number this is as applied to the edition of a book. If magazines were to *rain down*, and a man had only to pick them up like chips, it would take him a fortnight to pick up the copies of one single number, supposing him to pick up one every three seconds, and to work ten hours a day.

A portion of the edition of the Magazine, and also of the Story Books, are sent off in bales and boxes to booksellers and agents

View of the office where the Magazines and Story Books are mailed.

THE MAGAZINE CORNER.

who take them in quantities. Others are sent to individual subscribers by mail. The office shown in the engraving, which is situated in the back part of the great room in the Franklin Square building that contains the counting-room, is the place where these copies are addressed, and then mailed in bags sent from the Post-office to receive them.   Here, too, all the accounts are kept both of the Story Books and the Magazine.

The authors, whose writings the proprietors and conductors of this establishment bring before the public by the aid of the immense mechanical means and facilities they have at their command, and the still more immense business organization which they have built up, and which extends its ramifications to almost every city street and every rural village or mountain hamlet throughout the land, are very numerous, and they occupy every variety of intellectual and social position.   There are classical scholars who pursue their studies in learned libraries, and make profound researches into Greek and Roman lore.   There are intrepid travelers, who follow whales in the Pacific Ocean, or lose themselves among the fields and mountains of ice in the Polar Seas.   There are clergymen, who instruct the world with their expositions of Scripture, and of moral and religious truth; and statesmen, who discuss questions of politics; and novelists, who invent ingenious tales to furnish amusement and recreation for the weary and the solitary; and tourists, who give accounts of their tours; and embassadors, who relate the history of their embassies; and multitudes besides.   The productions of all these, and of many others, come into this vast establishment each in the form of a single roll of obscure and seemingly useless manuscript, and then, a few weeks afterward, are issued in thousands and tens of thousands of copies, beautifully printed, embellished, and bound, to instruct, entertain, and cheer many millions of readers.

THE END.

Printed in the USA
CPSIA information can be obtained
at www.ICGtesting.com
LVHW082056030823
754190LV00004B/250